TOÑO LIVES

porque domina todo

MELISSA KAY HERRERA

ISBN: 9798664618358 (Paperback)

*The names of some good people have been changed in this book. The names of some bad people too. It's for their own protection as well as mine. Cheers.

Cover Design: Hunter Herrera

Book Design: Selena Herrera

Author Photo: McKenzie Miller, https://mckenzie-luree-photography.ueniweb.com/

Printed by *junkbabe inc.* in the United States of America

First printing edition 2020.

junkbabe inc.

Millersburg, OH 44654

Acknowledgements

To hold this book in my hands and tell my readers, *"Here—read these words I bled over"* was a big ask from the book gods. This story is true. It tells the life of my husband, Antonio—who most know as George—and had to be pried from my very soul. When we met and fell in love so many years ago, he began to tell me piece by piece the life he had lived. Each story became lodged in my brain until there was no more room for it to reside. We knew that I would write a book about his life with its painful details intact. It took me longer than I anticipated. When you love the subject of the story you are soft with the content, not wanting to trample on the details. I grew a tough skin enough to give it what it deserved: rough edges, insight, and the revealing of horror-filled truths. It wasn't easy to write and I hope I've done it justice.

Be as gentle with it as I was, dear reader.

I am thankful for Julie Ruth who gave me the name of the Arquetopia Foundation and encouraged me to apply. They awarded me a writer's residency at their space in Oaxaca, Mexico in 2015—the very place much of this story takes place. I wrote the bulk of this book in that tiny room overlooking Oaxaca City. Thank you, Arquetopia. Find them at https://www.arquetopia.org/.

To the friends who kept asking me *"where's the book?"* over these many years, to co-workers and the readers of my newspaper column, my Twitter friends, and to everyone who simply told me they couldn't wait until it came out—thank you for pushing me.

To Lifeline, Breakfast Club, and Book Club who I talk to almost every day: you guys have kept me sane when none of us should have been. You know who you are.

To my entire extended family of nieces and nephews and cousins and aunts and uncles and brothers-in-law—I love you all.

To my mom and dad, who didn't live to see this book published—I finally did it. I miss you both.

To Eva, my husband's mom, thank you for bringing him into this world. Thank you for welcoming me into your home and for teaching this clueless white girl from Ohio how to make killer Mexican food.

To my sisters Jen, Lauri, Shelly, and Rhonda—thank you for continuing to ask me how the book is coming and for giving me a kick in the pants when needed. Thanks for the coffees and cakes and conversation all these years. You all knew it needed to be told.

A huge thank you to McKenzie Miller, my niece, who took my author photos. She knew exactly the look I wanted and did an amazing job. She also was one of my biggest cheerleaders and never failed to give me a push when needed. Check her out at https://mckenzie-luree-photography.ueniweb.com/.

To my editor Elaine Starner, what would I have done without you? You know exactly what you are doing when it comes to making a book come to life. With the simplest of fixes and rearranging, my book gained its voice. Your talent in editing is incomparable. Thank you.

And to my kids, my toughest critics, thank you. You are the beautiful culmination of dad's story, the long road he traveled filled with cold nights and tears. You are the dream he so longed for:

To Esabelle, my oldest, who I got to spend so much quality time with before the others came along. Thank you for the words I always needed to hear to move forward. You inspire me with your grit and determination and zest for living. I love our FaceTimes full of indignance toward current events (they keep me focused), and thank you for teaching me to think outside the box of the area you and I grew up in. I love you and Tyler so much.

To Selena, my middle baby, thank you for the long talks on theology and for showing me how to make the world a better place by spreading love. I so value our talks. Thank you for making the artwork for the front cover and for tackling the book design which was a feat—you knew exactly what I wanted. And in a twist of familiarity to dad and my love story, I am thrilled you found Sediq and will soon begin your life together.

To Hunter, my baby and soft spot, you are such a talented artist. Your college thesis film on a small portion of this book is a starting point, don't let it go. Your work on my book cover was the finishing electric pulse it needed. Our love for all things cinema and movies will forever be our bonding point. Thank you for bringing Dona, and very soon our first grandson, into our lives.

And finally, to my love, my Toño, my George—you crossed rivers to find me. Thank you for letting me tell the world your story. Even the hard parts.

for George,

who awakened me

and

filled my world

"No hay fuerza mas poderosa que la menta
humana,
quien domina la mente lo domina todo."
--Kaliman

*"There is no power stronger than the human mind,
and whoever dominates the mind dominates
everything."*
--Kaliman

Prologue

My fingers grip the iron underneath the train as the acid drips into my brain. The demon courses through me, and I can feel each wooden trestle reach up to grab me as I hold on, metal teeth like spokes in a wheel. The train is ready to swallow and reduce me to a mess of limbs and parts. Air, hot and filled with oil, hits me as I will my body to remain numb and nimble.

I am sixteen. I swing myself up into the train car rumbling over the tracks as the south Texas landscape scrapes raggedly by in my drug-induced haze. I stand on the edge of the train car and feel the wind whisper my name.

I am king, I think, *I am invincible.*

My hands grasp the heavy box-cutters as I check inside the stacks of boxes headed to nameless stores. Through the air the boxes go as I tumble them into the dark scrub, to be picked up later in unmarked stolen cars. *This is going to be a good haul*, I think too quickly, as a tingling lightly flicks my spine.

The black beast starts slowing down and grinds to a sudden halt. I see dark shadows scurry through the hot night. Immigration? I vault out the door and sharp rocks come up to meet me. I take off at a sprint.

In my years of sifting through endlessly moving train cars, I've never been caught. Their metal walls were as familiar and cold as a womb as I took items bound for nameless cities and towns. I've extracted items to be sold on dark, blood-stained street corners to shadow men, their organizations with names that would make your hackles rise. I'm paid with thick wads of cash, carefully counted out dollar by dollar. Drugs are part of the currency, stark and white. I stuff it into my pockets to divide, share, and consume later.

But right now, I sense more than see something behind me and hear the dog before I feel it. My head feels hollow, like a gaping hole ready to be split open. I feel the animal's breath on my neck as it's on me, reaching to take me down, mouth hungry and wide, trained to kill. I swing around and grab the dog with all I have, and I heave it until it lies limp.

Then they are on me—the men in uniform— and before I start to fade, my brain grasping for clarity, I think one thought: *God, please let there be more than this.*

This tale will be hard to tell.

1.

Most days when I think of my beginning, I find myself sitting on a beach in Puerto Escondido on the southern tip of Mexico. The sand sifts through my fingers and I can see my dad coming toward me with a wide smile on his face. His green army uniform makes him seem broader and stronger in my three-year-old mind. My older brother races beside him, and when they reach me, I find myself swinging through the air and landing in the waves of the Pacific Ocean with a splash. Up I swim until I break through the salty water that has penetrated my nose and makes me cough and spit. I know my dad is there to get me if I falter. This memory of him is strong and stays with me on days I can't remember much else.

Salt stings my eyes as I am enveloped by his embrace and the three of us walk back to the small house we have near the shore. My mom is waiting there in the kitchen. I can't think of my mom without thinking of her cooking. The smell of simmering beans or lentils with shrimp hits me with full force, and the taste lingers on my tongue. Even now, cooking equals love to me.

I only know what I had: my dad, my mom, my big brother Chucho, my little sister Maura, and my baby brother Porfirio. I was content with my bowl of beans and the comfort of home, the beach outside, and the toys I called mine.

What I didn't know was what my mom had suffered and how she had come to be with my dad in this home by the beach and the military base where he was stationed.

My mom was born Evangelina, and she came from a small village outside the town of

Nochixtlán called Apoala—a remote place in the lush but rugged southern terrain of the state of Oaxaca, Mexico. It is a place where tongues fly with the lilting language that is Mixtec, and where Spanish is a second language. It's a place where old traditions and superstitions live and kids are raised with the "be seen not heard" mentality. Hard-packed dirt paths lead through the village of small huts while adobe homes dot the landscape. She grew up knowing that her place was to learn to cook and to do it well. Laundry was done by hand at the river, as well as the grinding of the corn for tortillas with a metate, an unforgiving task that left the wrists strong, yet tender.

They were Mixtec, a people who are said to have inhabited the region as far back as 4400 B.C. By the time the Spaniards arrived in Mexico in the 1500s, this group of indigenous peoples had split into hundreds of different tribes. Proud, fierce, yet faithful to their land, they raised their children close to the home. Women were an integral part of village life, patting out large blue corn tortillas by hand and making sure the children were fed and clothed.

By the forties when my mom was born, the rugged village had yet to find progressive ways of thinking. Women were to fulfill their duty. My mom would recall that when she was ten years old, while walking to fetch water, she noticed she was bleeding. Thinking she was dying, she went back to her mom and asked her what was happening. Her mom beat her over and over and sent her away. She hadn't known that her period was starting. She was not taught things that should be known, and a girl's education, at best, was learned in the home. My mom never went to school or learned to read. She was bound by the hierarchy of village life where a girl's education wasn't a high priority. My grandpa, though, was a kind man who loved his daughter. Though poor and undereducated, life wasn't always so hard.

When my mom was older, in her later teens, she fell in love with a man named Rutilio, from her village. He was a regular in the market and liked to talk of hard things and people—of wars and historical figures from Mexico's bloody past. His eyes held violence, and he was well-versed in how to talk to a woman. Even though he was one year younger than my mom, she fell for him and his words of love. To be able to win her hand, it was necessary to bring an offering of wheat, corn, cigarettes, and several bottles of mezcal to the family. Patriarchy dominated the culture, and this was how a courtship proceeded. The only way to be with someone without your parents' consent was to run away with the one you loved, far enough away that the wrath of your parents couldn't reach you until it was too late.

The hard truth was that in a male-dominated culture you did what the man wanted you to do. Very soon my mom became pregnant at twenty years old with my oldest brother, Jesus, whose nickname is Chucho. When the realization dawned that she was pregnant, she went to Rutilio and told him she was having his child. They stayed together but were emotionally miles apart. He was heavy-handed, with a penchant for giving black eyes and violent blows to the gut. My mom, Evangelina, stayed on because that's what you did. You took what was dished out and persevered through the pain. You knew that he didn't mean those punches, and you got up every morning to cook breakfast with a smile.

Much later, we found out that Rutilio had fathered more children with women he had made pregnant, abused, and left. These facts came much too late to stop a wheel that was in perpetual motion. He left my mom pregnant and alone to have the baby and disappeared.

When Jesus was born on a spring day in 1965, Evangelina looked at him and hugged him tightly. My grandparents helped her as much as their meager funds could, but it wasn't enough. She left Apoala for the big city of Oaxaca to find what was there for her. Not long there, she met another dark-haired man with a crew cut and a wide smile. He was kind, and he was to be my dad.

My dad came from a town in Oaxaca named

Valdeflores. It was a dusty, rugged place that was meant for passing through. His past is somewhat of a mystery to me, with words and knowledge passed on by tongues that know part of the story. I only know he was born to Fausto and Patrona in 1938 and was born a higher class than my mom. In Mexico, she was considered *un Indio* (an Indian), low and unknowledgeable. If you felt this word stab you—*Indian*—then you know it is not used kindly. My dad's name, Maximo Herrera Ortega, meant one thing: His ancestors did not originate from Mexico, but from Spain. They would have descended from the conquistadors who took over the land and shaped it into their own version of Mexico. Our beloved and rugged terrain deterred yet never stopped the bloody melees from playing out. We were a conquered but never broken people. Over the years my dad's ancestors had melded together and by the time he was born, you would have been hard-pressed to tell that Spanish blood ran in his veins.

My dad was in the military, as natural to him

as blood pumping a beating heart. The military in Mexico is a fickle beast that spits out some of the best and wallows in its corruptness. But my dad felt a call to duty and joined the ranks of those soldiers, their cockiness worn on their faces like a badge of honor. He drove a green jeep that bumped and rocked over the haggard roads in the Oaxacan countryside. He went on maneuvers with his crew and became a colonel of highest regard.

He was a ladies' man, dark and handsome, so much so that women would throw themselves at him. Many longed to marry him and be his bride, and love and lust, when ignored, is a dangerous thing. Mexico is a land where superstitions run high and brujas (witches) sweep silently through dark streets. A foretelling or feeling, maybe a shivery premonition, is an easy thing to ignore.

When my dad, Maximo, met my mom, he was in his late twenties and ready to find contentment in his life. He wanted to settle down. My mom was petite, with flowing dark hair that ended below her bottom. She was everything he wanted in a wife. Embracing a woman who already had a child never fazed him, and he loved my brother like his own. My mom, running from her past, fell in love harder and faster than she should have. Was it because of being tossed away like she was nothing? Destiny had its way, and they got married.

Looking through the past is like a sheer curtain; you can see, but it's hazy and unclear. In the first years of my life, the curtain would be ripped away from my mom and dad's marriage. Life began gentle and would turn brutal.

I was born on a hot June day in 1967, under the Festival de San Antonio moon, and my name became Antonio Herrera Bautista, "Toño" for short. In the old tradition, many Mexican families name children after the saint on whose day their birthday falls. Calendars have a saint printed on each day, making it easy to choose a name for a child. My day was Antonio, which means *worthy to be praised*. I'm not sure that I deserved praise, but maybe a flicker of goodness was to be found in a name that flows from the tongue: Ahn-toe-nee-oh. Did you feel the letters slip gently off the tip?

There are so many things to remember from a mind so young, and most people don't remember them as they grow older. I find the memories just on the edges of where they've always been. I find that they are ever so slightly sliding off and out of my memory, and if I don't grab them, they will be gone. I test them and find them to be true. I gather them in my brain to bring out when needed.

My brother and I would play by the fire that consistently burned outside the house, shoving in sticks and throwing rocks at it to see what it would do. Bullets from my dad's gun seemed to be just the thing to put in a fire. Carefully we packed them around the edges of the flames and crept back to see what would happen. White hot explosions ripped through the courtyard. We giddily ran away, Chucho and I, to hide in the bushes until Dad came home. Mom came outside, frantically yelling our names; yet we remained hidden and together, sharing our naughtiness, until Dad came home to dole out a punishment that never quite came.

Naughty was a way of life for me. We liked to play on the base when we could, slipping in and around the sentries who tried to stop us from getting in. It was my dad's place, a place so exciting I had to be around where he was. One time, I was playing with a friend. I had a rope, and on the end had tied a piece of metal. I don't know what the metal piece was, but it was fun to twirl it around and around until I was dizzy, falling to the ground. My friend wanted to play, too, and I could see in his eyes that he was coming in to grab the rope. I hastily spun the other way, and as he grabbed it, the metal piece kept going. I woke up in the emergency room, a giant gash above my eyebrow. The scar remains, ragged and deep.

My mom gave birth to my sister Maura, and then my brother Porfirio. There were now four kids.

My dad suffered breaks in his mental faculties.

My mom believed he was slipping into madness. We couldn't figure out why one minute he was laughing and playing, and the next, his face turned dark and stormy.

Lust and jealousy grow like rampant weeds in Mexico and are something not to be toyed with. One day my dad didn't come home. Mom was frantic with worry because he hadn't been himself in a very long time. She suspected witchcraft.

Roll that around on your tongue before you swallow and banish the thought. Before I lose you here, stay focused. Witchcraft is prevalent in Mexico. Curses and spells run rampant in the lush countryside of my birth. Tales are told of the nahual, people who turn into animals, and witches who fly into your room at night to bite you and cast spells to trap ones they love.

My dad had cut ties with many women when he married my mom, but a wedding ring hadn't stopped what the women had felt. Some had been left angry and in pain, and when this happens, a visit to the local witch at the end of the street usually does the trick. Passion is a funny thing, and it can unravel in a fashion as dramatic as a telenovela. If that sounds trivial, then I can't change your mind. But evil exists on the backstreets and in small flickering shops where a pinch of this and that will do the trick.

The night my dad went missing was black as night. Animals nickered softly into the dark velvet sky as panic mounted. My mom and my uncle, who lived nearby, searched for hours in the dark streets, calling his name. "Maximo! Maximo! Donde estas?" And he was found many shivery hours later, naked and wandering alone in a nearby hamlet. His eyes were glazed, with pupils that were black as the deep end of a well. He didn't know who he was. The people who found him said, "Come and get him now. The devil is in him." And they brought him back home and laid him out on the bed.

Madness, when brought on by spells and chants whispered from frenzied hearts, is an ugly thing. Do you believe in this type of magic? In

Mexico, it is a way of life that is accepted before you grow up and know its true meaning. As he lay on the bed that night, dirty and smelling of ash and sex—smells I didn't comprehend—I stared into his eyes, eyes that didn't see me. I wanted to crawl into his arms, but he couldn't feel me. He was between worlds that weren't known to us, dark places that his heart seemed destined to run breathlessly through. My mom sat in a chair and wept, her eyes feverishly dark.

In between bouts of madness, he was still my dad. He would swing us high in his arms after maneuvers and run to the beach with us to stare for hours at the waves. He navigated two worlds, stepping on an invisible line that only he could see. My mom would pat tortillas high in a stack and we would munch happily on the beans and spicy salsa contained inside. If I could choose a feeling that described what I remember, it would be simply *happy*. I knew that things weren't right;

yet pushing that aside, I tried to be the best son I knew to be.

Being good didn't make everything okay, and my dad would disappear for hours at a time, especially at night. My mom would sit with us on the bed while we fell asleep, her face etched with worry that I couldn't seem to erase. I wanted to make her laugh, make those lines go away that signaled something wrong. I snuggled down deep in the bed with my brother and my sister at my side, my baby brother fussing at my mom's breast, and let the warm blankets lull me to sleep.

When you're small, moments rotate around those you look up to. We would take lunch to my dad at the base, and this routine would never waver. This memory is firmly ingrained in my mind. Mom would pack whatever she had made for lunch: tortillas filled with beans and cheese, caldo de pollo, sandwiches with yellow cheese, ham and spicy jalapenos, or bolillos filled with meat. In a round, tall tin that had three separate compartments, she would place the food and lock it up tightly. I wanted to be the one to carry the food, so most of the time I would grab the tin by the handle and take off at a sprint with my mom and siblings not far behind me. We did this daily, and Dad would always be waiting for us in the mess hall.

This day was no different than any other, as the sun reached its zenith in the middle of the blazing sky. I ran swiftly, tin swinging in my hand, around palm trees and down the path that would lead us to my dad and the military base. I stopped once to kick a lizard and examine it carefully but heard my brother and the others behind me. I wanted to be the first to reach my dad, so I pumped my legs as fast as my four-year-old body could go, food sloshing inside the tin. My heart was beating hard in my head as I slid into the gates with a wave at the guard, and he gave me a salute and a smile as I ran inside to the mess hall. Breathless, I turned the corner and came up short at the sight in front of me.

The mess hall was empty, and echoes from the heavy breaths I was taking filled the room, along with the surprisingly silent sounds of my dad dying. I remember the blood most of all, heavy and red, spreading out in a thick pool that glistened like so many sparkles in the sun. He lay face down in the middle of the floor, a ragged hole in his back where a bullet had torn through. If I close my eyes, I can see the gun lying beside him and the shredded pieces of flesh that pushed out the blood slower and slower. But his eyes — I can still see his eyes as they bore a hole right through me.

I knelt on the floor and looked at him, unable to speak. Those dark eyes, so like mine, imploring me to hear him, to know that he loved me. I felt as though his spirit entered me and caressed my soul, as his life slowly faded away, one drop of blood at a time. I know this to be true.

"Mijo, te quiero. Son, I love you."

Behind me, I could hear my mom and siblings

enter the room, and what I remember most is the screaming.

I wish I could gather all the pieces that are left of this day and tape them together into a cohesive collage. But I can't, and I swim deeply through a dark abyss to try and collect them. The days and months that followed my dad's death are ragged pieces of a dream. I don't remember burying him, and neither does my mom. I believe she has chosen to forget. I don't remember anything except finding him on the floor in a scarlet pool of blood that seeped slowly toward nothingness.

I remember that bolt of electricity that shot through me as I knew my dad was entering my consciousness. I feel that still today, that connection, that small slice of his soul that stayed with me. I don't know that I want to carry it, yet still it remains. The darkness he felt, that thing that overpowered him, was given to me. I battle it today. When I think of him, I feel love, yet a twinge of something runs down my spine. That darkness that took him. I feel it walking toward me in a straight line. I know it's him. I know he's there inside me as I move through my life. At times I still need him, yet know I need him to leave so I can breathe.

2.

It's always been thought that my dad's death was a murder, or at least those around me felt this way. Did he give in to the demon of suicide? I struggle to know because of how he held my eyes as his last breath was leaving him. If he loved us so much, why did he give in? Which way had the bullet entered him? The military gave us no answers, and I believe they are still floating around out there for us to find and gather and piece together. They told us they had gone on shooting maneuvers and came back. That's all they would say.

My mom nearly lost herself during this time. She consulted a white witch, who threw hot wax on the floor, awaiting answers inside the swirls it hardened into. Reading the wax, the witch said that Dad had had a curse put on him by a woman, but that wasn't how he died. She believed that he had been killed by jealousy inside army ranks, and that his ascent to a higher rank was stopped by someone killing him. Looking at my mom, she also saw that some of her children would die—but she could see no more.

The first memories I have after his death are of my mom rattling around in the kitchen, making tamales. I don't know how long after his death this was, months or weeks, I just know that she was bent on making those damn tamales and taking them to the market to sell. She told me to stay with my sister and watch over her. I don't know where Chucho was or where my baby brother was; I simply remember her telling me not to leave Maura's side.

"I want you to sit right here and make sure

she's okay," Mom said.

I climbed up on the kitchen table and sat next to Maura as my mom walked out the door. I looked at her face, and she was so still, so quiet. Her body lay perfectly still, and I bent my head down to listen for a breath that I knew wouldn't come. My sister was dead. Her small frame lay in repose on our kitchen table. She was three years old and I was four. I carefully watched her face and saw a small, white thing coming out of her nose. I pulled at it, then began yanking it, and it stretched further and further until the whole thing came out. This memory is what I have of her. It never leaves me, and I don't know why she died.

Weeks later, my baby brother, Porfirio, died as well. To this day, my mom doesn't remember how they died, but she used to. Sometimes she denies any of it happening at all. There have been lucid moments when she believes that it was witchcraft that killed them all, and just that quick, she remembers nothing. Her mind has stayed in a semi-defensive mode for over many years, and we can't pull her out of it.

Family comes out of the woodwork when crises arise, and soon my dad's parents stepped into the picture. They never had approved of my mom marrying my dad. She was an Indian. She was beneath him, they said. Now that he was dead, as well as two of their grandchildren, they decided it would be best to have my older brother Chucho and I live with them. They felt that my mom couldn't care for us. I don't know why my mom let us go with them to Valdeflores, or whether it was arranged against her will.

My grandma was a kind yet stern woman who fixed us hot drinks and fed us regularly. We would bounce a ball in the courtyard of her neatly kept home, as they were one of the wealthier families on their street. The interior was cool in the hot Oaxacan sun, and the exterior, though dusty, was swept and well-tended. Surrounding the home, in lieu of a fence, was a row of tall cactus that formed a formidable barrier to anyone who thought of entering. My grandpa was a kind man who would play with us for a little, then move on to whatever his day held.

My heart ached, and in the next second, I would go play. Four-year-olds have the capacity to feel deeply and know something is amiss, and in the next moment, be carefree. I was no different, but I missed my mom fiercely. Within months, my entire family had been ripped apart by death, blood, and pervading evil.

But I had my older brother, who was never very far from my side. We were like two peas in a pod, and we looked out for each other with a fierceness that was unmatched. He didn't take to my grandparents and was aloof and wary. They tried to make us feel at home with them, or as much as they could with the horrors that had befallen us.

One afternoon, Chucho came to me as I was bouncing a ball in the courtyard of the home and grabbed me and pushed me into a corner. He whispered into my ear, "I've seen Mom. She told me she is leaving on a bus to Oaxaca City this afternoon and wants us to go with her. Grandma isn't letting her see us. Watch for my signal to make a break for the bus stop. If you're not right behind me, I'm leaving you behind." My heart pounded out of my chest.

Our lives hold series of moments that you can recall like a flash of blinding sunlight. As my brother's words soaked into my four-year-old mind, the ache for my mom was like nothing I had ever felt. Chucho's eyes burned brightly as I stared into them. "Make sure you follow me."

I tried to act nonchalant, but I was four and began playing restlessly around the courtyard to pass time. Grandma made lunch for us and I ate, looking into her face to see if she could notice my nervousness. She cleaned up the plates and began to stack them neatly in the cement sink. She had lost her son. To madness? To what? Her brows furrowed, and I knew she held back pain as well as I knew she loved us fiercely. I didn't want to hurt her, but I wanted my mom. And I wanted my dad, and I wanted the dreams of blood and screams to go away forever.

Outside, I pressed my small body up against the adobe wall, which held the warmth of the sun. I could feel the heat on my skin as I picked up a spider and examined its many legs and curiosities. My head spun as a whistle, sharp and clear, came low at me through the cactus fence. I looked over to see my brother jumping through, slippery as a snake. He gave me a piercing look and was gone.

My heart started its pounding and I looked once again at Grandma in the kitchen, bent over the sink. I would never see her again. My gut felt a slow, sinking spiral and I turned and ran. I could feel her eyes on me as I slipped through the fence, cactus spines grabbing and holding me back. You know the feeling of someone standing behind you? That prickly sensation that sends shivers down your spine? The fence became a monster, not letting me through and holding onto me for dear life. My head and chest got through, but my legs became entangled and I couldn't move. I turned my head up the street and could see the bus waiting at the stop and I knew I wasn't going to make it—I knew my grandma would be grabbing me at any time.

I did not want to stay here. As I looked up in despair, I saw my mom and my brother stick their heads out of the bus and scream for me to come, to hurry.

I heaved my body, and the cactus let me go, as if it knew that nothing could hold me there. The bus was slowly pulling away, and as my little legs pumped faster and faster, my mom was screaming at the driver to wait just a few seconds more.

And then I was at the door and safe arms were pulling me in. We sank into our seats on the bus, my mom holding Chucho and me tightly, and the tears came hot and heavy until our clothes were wet with their aroma. I buried my head in my mom's chest and shuddered.

The path to take was not always clear to my mom, but she had her sons back and decided that the city of Oaxaca was where we needed to go. Down, down the winding road we went, the bus making slow turns in the very green and rugged terrain.

I don't know lots of details of this time, as my mom's memory has been mostly lost to the ravages of pain and time. I do know we found a small place to stay, but finding work and the means to keep going were not always easy. A woman alone, especially in that era, had a target on her back to be taken advantage of. *You need a place to stay? I'll rent to you, but for a price.* My mom was resourceful, but she had two small boys to care for and no one else to help. She did what she had to in order to keep her children alive.

Oaxaca is a biggish-small city. Three hundred thousand people inhabit the city central, and in Mexico that means most of them are out and about. Finding someone you once knew on those teeming streets is like finding a needle in a haystack. But it wasn't impossible. Somewhere in those desperate months that my mom was alone, as she tried to survive and keep us alive by any means, she met that needle in a haystack. A man from her past—the very one who had left her.

Rutilio.

When Chucho's dad reappeared on the scene, I had an immediate dislike for him. It was mutual. One day he came around as we were drinking licuados, and I looked at him and wondered why this man was talking to my mom. They had it planned, a way for us to meet him, and yet in his eyes I could see danger.

I don't know why my mom started a relationship with him again. I don't know how they found each other, but sometimes events line themselves up in a strange way, a way we can't fathom. My brother didn't know about him, had never met him. And me? I was the unwanted little piece of trash that was in the way. I was the reminder that "his woman" had been in a relationship with another man. He hated me because I wasn't his son. He hated me because I was another man's son. He had left my mom pregnant and alone. He had left her to move on to the next one and had never looked back. An abuser doesn't bring that fact up, he just reappears as though he never left—expecting everything to fall in line with his wishes.

At four years old, your main wants are your parents and to be able to play with carefree abandon. I had lost my dad in a terrible way, and here was another man—one who had already shown his true colors—barging into our already painful life.

I hated him.

In the beginning, I remember him trying. A few gifts here and there, maybe some tacos brought home in a paper sack, but mostly I remember moving in with him to an apartment that was bare. He worked as a security guard, and with his hard good looks, he was handsome in a complex way. At home, that faded away.

I implored her, "Mama, why do we need him?

We have each other. We don't need him." She
would gently pat my head and give me a hug
before returning to whatever task she was
performing. She seemed to blend into her role, as
though my dad had never existed. As though he
hadn't bled to death on the concrete floor of a
mess hall. I know now it was a defense
mechanism.

I was a child. I would play, then be upset when
his face darkened the door. We had been living
with him for several weeks when one day he
asked me to go buy charcoal for him. As little boys
will do, I dawdled and got sidetracked by a very
small zoo close to the Central de Abastos market. I
watched the animals and gleefully lost track of
time as they pranced around.

Then I raced home, forgetting the charcoal. I
knew there would be hell to pay. He started
chasing me as I neared the house, the rage heavy.
His wide Aztec face with the dark, dark
moustache bore down on me as I ran away from
him. Even though he was young and fast at that

time, I was still faster. Craftier. I jumped onto a wall and started running as he shouted after me with his eyes blazing. I kept running and running, and he never caught me.

When I became too hungry to stay away, I went home. He was waiting for me with blazing eyes. He had carefully arranged the caps of beer bottles on the floor, laid out neatly. I looked at him with challenging eyes.

"Kneel down on those caps," he said, with his dark eyes gleaming. I shrank back and started inching away. I could feel my mom somewhere in the house, hovering just out of my line of sight. His mouth spat a spray of dark spittle as he screamed, "I said kneel down on those caps!"

I started to run, and with hands of steel he grabbed me by the ear with pinching fingers— scars I still bear today—and violently shoved me down on the floor. The caps slowly started to sink into my knee caps, and the pain became a dull ache that increased to a roar. Blood started seeping out under the caps, in a slow, mesmerizing way, spilling drop by drop silently onto the floor. In the corner of the room he stood with his arms crossed, a look of silent victory etched on his face, the stench of beer breath in the air.

Barely able to breathe, I looked at him and promised myself then and there that he would never see me cry. Never. I would wipe the smirk off his face by his inability to scratch my surface.

When he finally left the room after many, many minutes, I rolled onto the floor with a thud. Hate filled me as I once again wondered why my mom could never save me.

If you have the guts and a no-quit attitude, you can always earn a living in Mexico. Rutilio didn't have that. He went through numerous jobs, and each time he came home drunker and drunker. At that point, he was a high-functioning drunk and could fool most people into believing he was fine. He talked of high things and dark histories filled with blood and war. He spoke of Benito Juarez with adoration in his voice, as most Mexicans do, but with more pride as Juarez hailed from Oaxaca—his state, his land, his tierra.

He worked at a parking garage close to the zocalo in town and used the uniform to appear higher than he really was. He was puffed up and cocky, yet I would call him coward. I could see how he was treating my mom, belittling her, berating, and especially punishing her for having a child who wasn't his. What would he have done, I thought, if my baby brother and my sister hadn't died? What would he have done with three children that weren't his? I tried not to let my mind wander to those places because nothing could bring back my family. Not even God, whom I implored with my childish wishes. "Father, please, I want my family."

I hated him with every cell in my body. I would talk to him in my mind and say, *"One day when I grow up, I'll tie you to the back of a truck and drag you through the streets. Then I'll take you to the top of a mountain and tie you to a tree and beat you with a whip until I'm tired or you die."*

These were the thoughts of a small, abused boy. One day I would make him fear me. I knew he would be nothing and do nothing that my mom would ever need, but she couldn't hear me. My voice was lost to her, and because of this, so was my childhood.

3.

We stayed in the city of Oaxaca for a time, but my mom and stepdad (I now called him stepdad) decided it was time to move north to Mexico City. I say "they" but really mean "he" decided to move us northward.

Their beloved Oaxaca was the only home either of them had ever known. It was beautiful, green, and when the mists rose in the morning, it was breathtakingly beautiful. But work and money don't always find you where you begin, so we went north, Chucho and I in tow, drug along in an endless spiral of upheaval. North, to find better work and a place to live.

The train we took chugged along on thin tracks that led through Oaxacan paradise and ever northward until the country flattened out just a bit in the central plains that surround Mexico City.

We settled in San Juan, Teotihuacán, the city of the gods, where the most beautiful pyramids of the sun and the moon rise along either end of the Avenue of the Dead. The town held its own beauty, yet to me, it never felt like home. A white house set in a small field awaited us, and we bedded down on the floor with petates and fell into a hard sleep.

When we awoke, I surveyed my new playground and immediately was filled with anger that he had moved us here. "Ma, why did we have to leave? Why?" The answer I had so hoped for would never quite come from her lips. My mom, so small in stature yet big in my eyes, had ridden along on the giant wave that he was, full of destruction, and could never get herself free of it. She looked me in the eye and told me to go play and find new friends. As I ran off, my stepdad watched me go, bitterness toward me overflowing from his heart.

New places fill most people with worry until they find their footing. Not me. I could make friends with most anyone and plunged into the neighborhood on a quest for friendship. We were nestled on the green side of Maquixco, a small colonia outside of Teotihuacán. There weren't many houses on either side of the road. A dirt road curved in front of the white house, and I set out on its path. A small river ran beside the path, set deeply down into a ravine. Its sparkling blue reminded me of good things, of the sea blue that was Puerto Escondido, and of my dad. The ache for him was fierce, yet I could feel him with me.

I didn't know where Chucho was that morning but found him soon enough, out and about playing with new friends and trying to fit in. Chucho was two years older than I, and he was my hero. We had never been apart, and I loved him like only brothers can love.

"Toño!" he cried. "I've been waiting for you."

I smiled and ran over to the group of friends who were kicking a soccer ball around. Off to the side of the group was a boy standing behind a tree, watching us play. His back was curved into a hump, and he wore a dusty backpack with a sad look to his eyes that told of days of pain and rejection. I ran over to him.

"Hi, my name is Toño. What's yours?" He looked at me like he wanted to hide, but I could see the curiosity and longing for someone to like him.

"Chon. Mi nombre es Chon," he uttered, looking down at the ground.

I smiled and said, "Come on, let's go play." His eyes looked watery and he hesitated, but I pulled his arm and smiled. The curve of his back was pronounced, and I was sure the kids made fun of him, but I could see the goodness in him and wanted to be his friend. He looked deep into my eyes and his face lit up. Chon had a donkey, I soon learned, and he liked to jump and fly onto its back like a superhero. He pretended to know Kung Fu, and we would reenact action scenes to take down the invisible monsters in our world. We soon became fast friends.

School is an inevitable thing when you're six years old, and as the first day of school arrived, I sat at the kitchen table and pouted.

"I don't want to go to school, Ma. Why do I have to?"

She looked at me and laughed as she split open bolillos and took out the soft insides. Spooning a thin layer of black beans inside the crusty roll, she said, "Because you have to. It's your job. You'll be fine, mijo. Do your best."

Chucho looked at me from his seat across the table and shook his head. "Let's go, or we'll be late. I don't want to be late on the first day," he said, urgency in his voice. Chucho loved school.

Mom packed our lunches and shooed us out the door. The sun was shining, and as usual I was dawdling. School seemed like the worst choice for me on this sunny day, and soon I could barely see Chucho ahead of me on the path. He turned around and yelled at me to hurry, but I picked up a stick and started dragging it behind me, making lines in the soft dirt. Chucho was the one who always did things the right way, though I was braver than he—or at least, I thought myself to be.

The path stretched out through a thicket of pines, and with the river to my side, I kept trudging onward toward what I knew would be a terrible waste of my day. When I finally saw the school come into sight, I stopped and stared at the frame of it. My brain rattled around for a bit and I knew I wouldn't go in.

Instead, I turned myself toward town. We were still new to the area and I hadn't yet been able to explore. I found myself in el centro.

I walked around in circles and sat for a while in the gazebo in the center of el jardin. In most Mexican towns and villages, the heart of the city has a garden, or jardin, that is the center of town life. It's where you go to sit and watch the people go by, where the shoe shiners set up their business, and where lovers go to kiss the minutes away.

I surveyed San Juan, Teotihuacán, and didn't quite know if it felt like home yet. The mercado was bustling with vendors and women scurrying around with their bags filled to the brim with vegetables and fixings for the afternoon meal. Steam rose from vast pots of atole, coffee, and towel-covered pans filled with tamales. My stomach rumbled even though breakfast was still in my belly. I meandered through the mercado, taking in the sights and sounds.

Little boys, though, have a short attention span, and soon I walked back onto the main square and where many colorful buses were parked in haphazard rows. Drivers were hanging out the doors, yelling their destinations so people would know which bus to catch. My interest piqued, I slipped onto a bus while the driver wasn't looking and found myself in rows of tall seats filled with people. No one was paying attention to me as I filed past all the seats to the back of the bus. I had been around buses before and had seen people climb aboard and sing for a few pesos.

Always thinking about how I could earn money, I opened my mouth and started belting out some rancheros that I had heard on the radio. Lost in the song and the smiles of the people, I didn't hear the door shut or feel the bus move forward. I wasn't exactly sure what was happening, but soon realized that the scenery in the scrubby landscape of this area was flying by. I ran to the front of the bus, but it was too late—we were already moving.

I was afraid to tell anyone I was on the bus alone, so I grabbed onto a seat and stood while the bus took me toward who knows where. Buses are a major mode of transportation in Mexico, and many stops are made as the bus slowly fills up with sitting people as well as people standing in the aisles. I slowly became invisible. I shrank into myself and watched the road ahead. I didn't want anyone to notice me and tell my dad, so I would get into trouble.

If I'm truthful, I wasn't scared because this was an adventure. Not going to school was the best choice I had made that day. We sped through towns and small villages and chugged up tall hills that were populated heavily with people and houses.

Soon, a huge city came into view and I gazed in wonder at as many houses as I had ever seen at one time. The bus pulled into a terminal, and if you've ever been to Mexico, you know you'd better grab your stuff and get off because there is no waiting.

I tumbled out and looked around me at masses of people coming and going. Vendors lined the fence outside a building, shouting, "Quesadillas! Tacos! Memelas!" My stomach rumbled as I walked by each tiny place, their piles of good food steaming in the air. Past them, I could see tracks and trains and I knew we were at a station. *I know where I am*, I thought. *This is how we got to the new place we live.* I was excited at this realization, yet worried how in trouble I would be when I got back and they found out I had never made it to school.

I may have been little, but I was smart. Believing in myself has always come easy, and I found a way to get past the soldiers with their guns, who are found at most public areas of transport, as well as the ticket agents. I found myself near the tracks where people milled about waiting for their train to arrive. It was a busy place, where everyone minded their own business with their heads down; no need to notice a small boy slipping up the steps and onto the first moving train that pulled in.

My heart pounded as I wedged myself in and under the last seat. I would wait here until the train stopped in my town, and as the engines roared to life and started to move, I was lulled to sleep by the rocking of the big beast as it carried me forward.

I woke with a start, the train moving liltingly beneath me. My bones ached with the position I was in, and I stretched a little bit at a time until I could pop my head out and look up and down the aisles.

My mom always said not to stretch my bones, or the devil will be able to get me, but that's the way superstitions go in Mexico. I would find out that this may have been the truth and the devil was on my tail, if you believe in that sort of thing. I had learned that evil exists and can follow people all the days of their lives. I quickly got up and found the train car to be sparsely filled. People were resting with their heads back on the seats, and the conductor was nowhere to be found.

I slipped out the back door of the very last car and looked around. As the landscape flashed by, I could see that it looked nothing like where we had moved to in Maquixco. The scenery was very green, and the air was hot. The train slowed as we pulled into a small station for more people to get on. Vendors got on the train to peddle their wares. Baskets were filled with sweet bread, candies, and peanuts, and pans jiggled with gelatinas—brightly colored layers of goodness.

I looked into their faces and could hear their accents and knew I was not heading in the right direction. I knew then I was going farther and farther away from my mom and my brother. The train chugged to life, and I hid myself on the steps of the caboose so the conductor, coming through to punch the new travelers' tickets, wouldn't find me.

After it was safe, I slipped back in and took a seat while scrunching myself into small ball so as not to be seen. I looked out the dirty train window to watch the scenery change to a verdant landscape. The train stopped several more times in little villages and hamlets, and more vendors got on and got off in a succession of wonderful smells and sights.

Each time, I hid until the coast was clear, and

each time I was successful in my bid to stay hidden. I learned that I was crafty and could do things most people couldn't. The fear of being gone hadn't yet hit me, and the only thing I feared was the wrath of my stepdad when I did make it home. At this point, I didn't know when that would be. I laid my head against the window and fell asleep, not knowing where this path would take me.

I woke to the train clashing and banging to a stop. People were gathering their things and forming a line to get off the train. We were at the end of the line—and I had no idea where I was. As people disembarked, I jumped off the steps and ran onto the platform, so no one would see me and I could merge into the mass of people inching forward into the station and out onto the street.

I looked around and took in a city that looked familiar, yet when without the safety of your parents, looked unfamiliar. I started walking and walking, buildings and people passing by me, and I became weary, so weary. I stopped on a street corner to rest, and emotions I'd held inside overcame me. Tears formed in the corners of my eyes, and putting my head down, I let them come, hot and salty.

I was lost. Unequivocally lost in a city that seemed vaguely known to me, but all I could do was see my mom's face in my mind, her hair as thick as thread and black as night, holding out a cup of atole to me in the morning to drink. I could see Chucho urging me to hurry as he turned his head and followed the correct path, his disappearing frame in my hazy memory. He was always responsible in listening to Mom.

Where was I? What would I do? Why didn't I listen?

As the tears fell wet on my cheeks, my small frame shook with wracking sobs. Someone tapped me on the shoulder, and I looked up with heavy eyes. "Que paso, hijo?" a kind lady said as she put her hand on my shoulder. "Are you lost?"

I shuddered inside as I realized that I would be in big trouble if the police or anyone found out that I was alone. "No," I said. "I'm okay. I lost all my money to get home and my mom will be mad at me." The lie slipped out smoothly and quickly.

Compassion shone in her eyes as she fished her coin purse out from underneath her rebozo and handed me one peso. "Here, take this. Now get yourself home so your mom won't be worried."

She smiled and carried on her way as I looked at the coin in my hand. My emotions warred within me. I felt bad for lying, but my instinct to survive was stronger. I didn't know where I was in this world, but I wasn't going to let anyone put me in jail for leaving and not going to school. If I learned how to make money and fend for myself, I could make it. I didn't yet know how resilient I really was.

4.

What I didn't know at the time was that the bus had taken me from my home in San Juan, Teotihuacán, to Mexico City, where I had boarded a train to Oaxaca, Oaxaca. I had traveled through two states to the town we had left to move northward not that long ago.

My little mind was working overtime just to know what to do each second and minute that I was away. How to eat and how to not get caught—that was a priority, or so I thought. It turned out I was just another kid on the streets.

I took that one peso the lady had given me and

walked until I came upon a mercado where I smelled delicious things steaming from pots and frying on grills. My stomach growled hungrily, and I bought several tacos from a lady who had a kind face. "Can I have one order, please?" I said in my best-behaved voice. She looked at me hard and started placing small corn tortillas on the grill to warm, then threw some finely chopped meat to char for the tortilla. She gently placed the meat in the corn tortillas and topped it with onion, cilantro, and a spicy green salsa.

"Fifty centavos" she said, as she handed me the plate. I ravenously grabbed it from her, paid my bill, and waited for the change. The warm tacos melted in my mouth as I inhaled them quicker than I could think.

Just down from her was a vendor who sold milkshakes, and I sat on the high stool and ordered. "Chocolate, por favor." The liquid went swiftly into a blender and soon I was sipping on my favorite beverage. It went down my throat cool and tasty.

After my stomach was filled, I set out to explore my surroundings. The zocalo beckoned me with its lights and sounds and the beautiful green trees that shaded the square. Lovers and friends lined the benches that were placed on the hard concrete, and kisses and laughter could be seen and heard emanating from all corners. Mexico wears its passions on its sleeve, and public displays of affection are the norm. Tamale and churro vendors cried out as they walked around selling their wares, and I was so mesmerized by the sights that I didn't notice the sun had set and it was nearly night. A shiver ran up my spine as I realized that I had no place to sleep. I was lost.

My mind thought back to that same morning when I was safely sitting at my breakfast table, complaining about going to the first day of school. My mom and my brother, who were everything to me, were probably so worried and not knowing where to look for me. I was sure my stepdad didn't care one bit. Today, when I ask them, they say that they searched high and low for me, in every alley and in every corner they could think of. I was nowhere, and in rural Mexico 1973, there was no way to get the word out, or at least none that they could think of. My mom was in shambles and there was no recourse.

As it grew darker and the square started clearing out, I worried about what to do. I decided to go back to the mercado where I had eaten.

My feet were weary from walking and also from the rubber shoes that I had worn that morning. My stepdad didn't think new things were necessary for me, so he had found a pair of rubber slip-on boots and made me wear those. Earlier in the day, my feet had squished around in them, the sweat of the day permeating each step. I wrinkled my nose at the smell, because even though small, I sensed that staying clean and presentable would help me get further. Appearance was key to the way people treated you, and if you smelled, it was not a good thing.

I walked those boots closer and closer to the mercado until I spotted some tables that were cleaned up and had chairs stacked on top of them. It was the dark side of the market, but I puffed out my chest and told myself not to be afraid. *I'm alone*, I thought, *but I know my dad and God are watching me. I'm sure they're sitting right across the street and will keep me safe.*

I peered under the darkened shadows of the table and decided this was the place. Scurrying under and curling into a ball, I saw a stack of old newspapers lying nearby. I grabbed a few sheets and covered my body as best as I could. A chill ran through me as I felt the cold concrete penetrate my skin, and hot tears pricked my eyes. I pulled the newspapers closer and covered my face and asked God to put me to sleep.

I woke to clanging pans and people talking. Coffee smells filled the air, and I quickly slipped out of my hiding place under the table. I heard a "Hey, what are you doing under there?" yell as I scurried away to sit on the edge of the street and consider what my next step might be.

My bladder was yelling at me, I was hungry, and the magnitude of what had befallen me was beginning to sink in. I checked my pockets and felt a few small centavos left there from the day before. Down the street I could see a church, and not knowing where else to turn, I shuffled toward it. The streets seemed vast and wide, and my head spun with hunger and restless thoughts.

As I entered the courtyard of the church and looked up at its tall spires, thoughts formed in my mind that I needed to get out.

"God, I know that I didn't listen to my mom and my brother. I'm lost, and I don't know which way to go. I'm going to put these last centavos in the offering because it's all I have. I know if I do, you'll take care of me." I believed this, like a trusting child knows that his parents will always feed him or that the stars will always appear in a darkened sky come nightfall. My faith at six years old is something that has never left me. I don't know why it was so strong, but God knew, and I knew he would take care of me—no matter what I had to do to survive.

As I walked out of the church after giving my entire being to God, I felt much better. I knew I could survive, and I knew I must do it well.

Which brings us exactly to what life is like living on the streets when you're little. People don't really see you, unless you do something to make them notice. As kind and open as my people are, they are also busy and full of errands and work to get to. Shoulders wrapped with bright shawls, dark-haired heads carrying baskets with unknown contents, and hard work-booted men walked the streets on their way to whatever their day held. A small boy, hungry and tired, didn't make much of a blip on their radar.

I remembered how I had cried when I first arrived and the lady had given me the peso. Those had been real tears that day—nothing made up. I knew that if I did that again, I could gain compassion from passers-by wondering what was wrong with me. I found a busy street corner and looked around stealthily at the crowd. No one was noticing me as I leaned up against the corner, dabbed saliva at my eyes, and pretended to cry. I made my body shake with the effort, and it wasn't long until several people had stopped to ask me what was wrong. Don't change what works, I always say, so I fed them the line of losing my money to get home and that my mom would be so angry with me. I soon had a pocketful of pesos, and my whole world opened up because I knew then and there that I would be okay—no matter what.

I performed this "trick" every day on different street corners, and the results were always the same. At night, I would crawl under the table in the market, cover myself with newspapers, and fall restlessly asleep. I tried not to think about my family and what they must think. I felt that they would try to find me, but didn't know if they had any idea in which direction I had gone. They might think I was kidnapped and give up hope. I knew to give up hope was to give up completely, and I couldn't do that.

Every day was different, and I found that it took little money for a boy my size to make it. When my pockets were full, I would buy my favorite sandwiches and chocolate shakes, telling myself that I deserved them. I worked hard to cry for that money, and I was hungry.

Besides being a tourist destination, the square of Oaxaca boasts many fine hotels and restaurants that have covered patios and outdoor seating. I would see the many Americans sitting outside, eating their bagels, jam, and cream cheese in the morning along with a cup of steaming coffee. I tried every morning to comb down my hair and wash the best I could at various places I could find water, although it didn't help my appearance and clothing. I would saunter up to these outdoor tables with the piles of food left on them by customers and snatch morsels as quickly as I could. The food was magnificent and gave me a taste for what the rich people ate. *If they can eat it, so can I*, I thought. *Why do I deserve any less?*

I never wanted to seem less in anyone else's eyes, so I became even more crafty and charming. Sometimes the waiters would come after me, not being able to yell in a very public restaurant, but I was swift and got away from them before it was too late.

I knew my clothes were starting to be very dirty and that being dirty would get me nowhere. I began to steal clothes off lines or a pair of underwear from the heaping stalls in the market that sold clothing. Shoes as well could be quickly taken while purchasing something else smaller, like socks. When the vendor reached for the socks, you swiped the shoes—voila! It was magic, and I was so fast they never caught me. I was able to stay in partially clean clothes because of this, but living on the hard concrete tore them to shreds, and I always looked ragged no matter how hard I tried to stay presentable.

I decided in my mind that it was okay to steal because I kept giving to the church. Wouldn't God forgive me? One day when I went into the church foyer where the container was to drop coins in, an old shawl-covered lady was in front of me. She padded slowly to drop her coins, and I saw that she held in her hand only a few centavos. She looked at me with piercing yet kind eyes and said, "It's all I have. If I don't give it to God, how will he help me?" She put her hand on my head as she shuffled out of the church and I could do nothing but stare at her. Was she an angel sent to relay a message to me?

To this day, I believe she was. I knew I was right and that I wouldn't be forgotten, lost and alone on the streets of Oaxaca. But I wouldn't feel sorry for myself. Never. I would get up daily, comb my hair, wash my face, and keep going— even if it killed me.

Click, clack, CLICK, CLACK! My eyes shot open blearily in my space underneath the table. Purple high heels swung back and forth, hitting the edge of the table with a force.

"Hey, papi, no quiere ir conmigo?" I heard a sultry voice call out to a man walking by.

The clicking continued until finally I crawled partially out from underneath the table, hit those purple shoes as hard as I could, and in stern voice said, "Get off my table!"

I saw the purple shoes jump off so quickly that I thought she would fall. She peered under and looked at me carefully, dark eyes taking me in.

"Baby, what are you doing under there? Come out and let me see you."

I slowly slid off my blanket of newspapers and crawled out into view.

"Pobrecito, why are you sleeping under there? Are you hungry?" she said, as my stomach howled in protest. "Come with me," she said soothingly, with no room for argument.

She held my hand as we walked toward the corner of the street to a taco stand with a lone light hanging above it, the only stand open this late at night. There were a few men eating tacos and drinking beer, and they looked at us as we boldly walked up to order.

"You want tacos? I'll get you tacos. Give us a whole plate, please."

The men looked at us, and low and slow catcalls issued from their tongues, greasy with the taste of tacos.

"What are you doing with that kid?" they asked, silently looking her up and down.

"Mind your own business, hijos de la puta," she spat, as she put her arm around me. I shuddered at her touch because for weeks no one had touched me or caressed my face with loving hands. I was slowly dying inside from loss of human contact, but my stubbornness kept me going.

Tears sprang to my eyes as the tacos were handed over and she led me to the sidewalk, where we sat on the curb. I gobbled down the tacos and a soda that she had bought as well.

"Honey, why are you alone here at night?" she asked.

I looked down at my plate and didn't know

what to say. I was afraid to tell her, afraid she would turn me in. But when I looked up into her face—blue eye shadow on her lids, black kohl eyeliner heavily outlining her almond-shaped eyes—I could see past the façade and saw that she might really care. Maybe she could help me? Trust didn't come easily and I was wary.

She smiled as she saw my confusion over what to say and said, "No worries, mijo. Let's go back to my place, and you can stay with me for a few nights. Come on."

We returned the plate and glass bottle to the vendor and continued on down the street until we came to a smaller street lined with small doors. Behind each door was a room that held a bed, table and chair, and a small stove. She told me I could lie down here until she needed the room, and then she stepped out the door and went back to work.

I fell deeply asleep, not having slept in a bed for what seemed like forever, and was soon awakened by her coming into the room with a man. She smiled at me and told me to sit outside on the steps until she was done. I sleepily sat on the stoop with my head in my hands, and as the door closed behind me, I could see her taking her clothes off piece by piece. I quickly turned my head as my senses pounded with what I'd just seen. Strange sounds started seeping out under the rickety door frame, which soon turned into moans that sounded like someone was being hurt. Should I peek in and make sure she was okay? I was afraid to, for fear of what I would see; but not long after, the door opened and the man stumbled out, buckling his belt and giving me a wicked grin. "One day, when you grow up," he said to me, flicking me a coin. "Tell your sister she was really good."

She popped her head out and told me to come back inside, but I was shy and looked at her with enough curiosity to make her laugh and grin.

"It's okay, baby, this is my job. All I want you to do in exchange for sleeping here a few nights is to stand watch while I'm working in here. Let me know if anyone is coming or tries to get in," she said. "But for now, let's go to sleep. I'm done for the night."

She lay down and motioned for me to come to bed. I lay down beside her, thoughts of what I had seen and heard on my mind, but then she put her arm around me. Soft snores came out of her mouth, and I snuggled in just a bit further, feeling the warmth of a human body beside me for the first time in days. I thought of my mom, and cried myself to sleep.

5.

Say the word *prostitute* and you get wrinkled noses and rolled eyes, words that are judgmental and condescending all in one turn. The women I encountered chose a hard life when there were no other choices. For me, they were the angels of the night. I have never met anyone kinder or more willing to help me than these beautiful ladies who would throw their heads back and laugh throatily until tears came to their eyes. They were a salty and brave and took nothing from the men who used them unless it was their money. They took care of me when I didn't know what else to do.

There came a day, though, when a hard knocking nearly blew down the door and caused a tremor to roll through me.

"Hey, open this door and get out here, hija de la chingada!"

She took one look at me and held her fingers up to her lips in a silent shush and mouthed, "Don't say a word." She cracked open the door in an attempt to block entry but it didn't work, and the door flung open and a man in a fedora barged in and looked me up and down.

"What the hell is he doing here?" he screamed. "The guys were telling me you had some kid living with you. He needs to get out!"

She looked at me tenderly and eyed him with daggers. "He was hungry and needed a place to sleep for a few days, pobrecito," she said. "What's it to you?"

He looked at me coldly and proclaimed loudly, "He better be gone when I get back."

He slammed out the door with her screaming behind him, "Or what? Or what? Pinche pendejo."

Her face was red with anger yet resigned to something I didn't understand. I didn't know the girls were "managed" and that he was their "manager" and didn't take kindly to them looking motherly. It took away from their job and how men—potential customers—looked at them, which in turn took money out of his pocket.

She cupped my chin and said, "Don't worry. You can stay another night, but that will have to be it."

The pat on my head felt hollow as my heart sunk to my stomach. Sleeping in a bed the past few days had felt so nice, so cozy—but I knew it couldn't last. If he came back, he would hurt me. I knew that.

She was staring into space, and I wondered if she had kids of her own, or wanted kids. Maybe helping me took her back to what she had lost? Even though I had witnessed too many things while staying with her, sights and sounds that would never leave me, she was kind and she cared for me. I saw that men were animals, at times—in other ways than my stepdad was—and I swore I would never turn out like that.

I didn't want her to get in trouble, so I told her I would go out and get some sweet bread for breakfast. She nodded her head and went to make some coffee in preparation, while I slipped out the door—never to see her again.

I learned hard and quick not to become attached to anyone. It hurt less if you didn't care about someone's feelings, especially your own. Love hurt, love left, and it didn't care when it ripped your whole world apart chunk by chunk. I had been torn away from my family by my own two feet and decided that I wouldn't ever let anyone get close to me ever again. I didn't need anyone. I would only take what I needed to get by.

The 20 de Noviembre market in Oaxaca held many wonderful smells. It was where I first laid my head down at night, and it was where the vendors slowly learned to know me as Toño, the boy who was simply there. I had a quick smile and was charming, and it didn't seem to take long for the moms who worked the food stands to like me. I would saunter up to them and grin. "Do you have an atole for me?" My brown eyes would sparkle, and my teeth would slowly start to show through a crooked smile. They couldn't resist me and I knew it. Soon I had a hot drink and a sweet bread to dip into it.

There were many kids who came with their parents to the market, and they eyed me carefully before talking to me. I'm not shy and looked back at them just as carefully. No words seemed necessary as we eyeballed each other throughout the weeks, and soon we were all playing like we had been friends forever. Miriam, Rebecca, Maria, Socorro, Jorge, Ricardo, and others were soon a part of my clan, my gang, my crew.

I would wake up in the morning and sneak into the restroom to wash my face and body—at least where I could reach—and would sit on the curb and wait for them to get there. Sometimes they would find me before I was up, and I would be embarrassed at my little nest, knowing their faces had been washed by their moms and their clothes were clean. But they were my friends and they didn't care.

I knew each stall where their parents sold food, as well as which ones would feed me. Finding food was always high on my list, and breakfast plus lunch could easily be had at one of those places. I was polite, even though I looked a little dirty, and tried to endear them to me in ways I knew would benefit me in the long run.

One of the little girls, Maria, was my favorite. She was so beautiful in my six-year-old eyes that I acted the fool at times to get her attention. A moment that sticks out for me was when I saw her talking to another little boy. They were sitting on the sidewalk curb, and I felt jealous that she would talk to him and not to me. My head spun around as to what I could do to get her attention. Girls like boys that can do lots of crazy things, right? What if I ran as fast as I could in front of them and jumped really high! I looked at them sitting there, and without thinking it through, I started running. Faster and faster I hurtled toward them with thoughts of grandeur in my head. *She's going to love me even more because of how fast I am!* As I approached them, I took a giant leap and sailed over them, knowing that I would clear them both and reach the street with a smooth drop. My plan was to turn around and smile at them and walk slowly away like the coolest of boys.

Instead, what happened is something I'll never forget for as long as I live: As I was jumping over them… I farted. Long and loud. So embarrassed, I kept on running and never looked back. I don't know if they laughed at me or were so shocked that they didn't know what to say. All I know is that I didn't turn around and I never talked about it again to them, though Maria always stayed my favorite.

Like a pack of wild dogs, we boys ran in and around the markets. The ladies who ran their food stations would yell and chase us until we turned and faced them, a big smile on our faces as they scolded us and smiled. Some days, we pretended to be cowboys and Indians, and we used pretend whips and horses. Sometimes I actually herded up stray dogs and tied ropes to them to pretend they were mine—I believed myself a dog whisperer. Battles were held with the kids who inhabited other markets nearby. We fashioned swords and other weapons to have a battle royale. It was mayhem in the market center as we shouted, battled, and created chaos around the stalls. The people in charge ran after us, but we were too swift and got away, grinning as we went.

After these wild charades, we would head down the street to the local radio station and settle in to listen to the radio shows they aired every afternoon. We could listen outside as the station broadcast out onto the street for all to hear. I always arrived one hour early to hear the live bands, who were hoping to become famous and played by the radio station. They would play right up until it was time for the main event. We heard stories of Vaquero and Aguila Solitaria, of knights and damsels in distress. But my favorite show of all time was Kaliman.

Kaliman was a mystical man from the east who could leave his body while meditating. His telepathy, in particular, fascinated me. He would have long adventures, dole out sage advice, and be so fascinating while his soul was traveling the world. His trusty helper, Solin, would watch over his body while he slept. It made me think of Chon. My favorite saying of Kaliman's was, "Que domina le mente, domina todo. *If you can control your mind, you can control everything.*" I hung onto every single word Kaliman said—he was my hero, you see. He was able to take situations and things and turn them into good just by having and using his knowledge. I digested every piece of wisdom he put out there, as I sat on the cold concrete on the streets of Oaxaca. Kaliman would come to mean so much to me—his knowledge and words—that even though he was just a fictional character, he helped me make it when I could no longer bear being on my own. I knew that if I could be like him, I could make it—just concentrate and use your mind and you'll be okay. I would read his comic books as well and gaze into his deep blue eyes, thinking about my dad who had died. My body stiffened, and I became resolute yet again to my circumstance. I had no one to take care of me but me. Kaliman's words held even more power.

"I am Kaliman," I whispered.

At home, I learned later, it was a maelstrom of quiet chaos. When I disappeared, they didn't know where to look. The white house by the river became a prison for my mom and my brother. They wept and grieved and tried to look for me wherever they could. But they didn't have the means for a large-scale search, and they suffered silently because of one thing—my stepdad, who wouldn't allow them to search further. Every time my mom would want to search for me, he would say, "He's not there. You won't find him. It's time to let him go." His dreams of me not being around had come true. He didn't care that I was gone. That my mom and my brother cried every day meant nothing to him.

My brother ached inside and suffered because he thought it was his fault that I was gone. "I told him to hurry — he didn't listen. I don't know where he went," he would say to my mom as they cried together silently. I try to imagine, now, what I would do if one of my kids was missing. I would go to the ends of the earth to find them. I would turn every rock upside down until I could go no further. But in 1973, there were no means for someone from rural Mexico with an angry, abusive husband. What could she do?

When fear is present, I believe evil manifests itself in ways we don't want to see. My brother tells a tale of a night at the white house, several weeks or months after I disappeared. All was quiet save for the sheep bleating softly outside the window, and my brother lay quietly sleeping as the minutes ticked into the dark night. My mom and stepdad were asleep and snored into the heaviness of the night.

Out of his dreams Chucho was awakened by a voice, crying urgently to come and help him. Shivers went up his spine as he lay in a deathly quiet pose, listening with ears even more intent. *Maybe I was dreaming*, he thought, but no—*there it is again!*

He got up quietly and crept to the wooden door that was poorly constructed and let in moonlight and wisps of cold air that permeated the room. He put one eye to the cracks in the door, then listened.

"Help me! Help me, Chucho!" A voice carried from down the embankment and near the river. He froze as he recognized the voice—it was Toño! He had come back and couldn't find his way to the house! He ran over to Mama and shook her awake.

"Que paso, hijo? What's going on?" she asked.

Chucho shivered violently as he whispered, "Toño is here! He's outside crying for help and can't find his way to the house! We have to go get him!"

The look that passed over my mom's face was one of hesitant hope, and she got up to look out the door.

At the same time, my stepdad awoke and grumbled for everyone to get back in bed.

"No, Pa, Toño is here! He's outside crying for us!" my brother said, trying to make his dad understand.

My stepdad got up as well and stumbled over to the door. He opened it and stepped outside into the blackest night he had seen. The moon was low and covered by clouds as he walked several paces out and listened. Soon, a piercing yet low groan drifted up from the river along with the same cry for help Chucho had heard. My stepdad looked back at my mom and my brother standing in the doorway and turned to walk to the edge of the embankment. His eyes, adjusting to the sparse light the moon was giving off, peered over the edge to see where the noise was coming from.

"Toño, estas aqui? Are you here?" he said gruffly, yet soft enough not to carry through the night air. He could see a figure down by the water, walking slowly, almost floating. *Are my eyes playing tricks on me?* he thought, as he squinted to see who the figure might be.

The moon, suddenly bright as the clouds parted, shone beams on the edge of the water and he froze, stock still, and took in the sight that was before him. Shrouded in white, he could plainly see that it was a woman walking listlessly by the water. Her dress drug on the ground behind her as the words emanated from her lips in a voice that was not her own—in a voice that belonged to a six-year-old boy who was lost. "Help me! Help me! I can't find my way home!"

My stepdad could see her starting to turn her head around and he turned quickly, his spine rippling with chills, and ran back to the house where they were waiting. "Get inside right now!"

he cried, as their faces turned to confusion.

"Who is it? Where's Toño?" my mom and my brother cried in unison.

"Shhh, don't make a noise," he whispered as they sat inside, terror etched on their faces.

They could hear a shuffling come from outside as the woman made her way closer and closer to the small adobe home, and when she reached as close as she could come, a small voice cried in Toño's voice yet again, "Why won't you help me? I want to come in! I've been gone so long."

My brother was paralyzed by fear and confusion, not knowing why they couldn't open the door. My stepdad held his finger to his lips and told them, "Don't look out the cracks of the door. You must not see her face. If you do, she will take you."

At that moment they knew what my dad had seen—what was hovering outside our house. La Llorona, the most feared specter in Mexico, was using my voice to trick them. It's said that La Llorona is beautiful, ethereal, even, from behind;

but if you see her face, you will perish because it is a haggard disarray of ugliness. She will take you with her and end her prison sentence, which is to eternally walk the earth as punishment for drowning her children in a river.

My mom wept internally, and Chucho covered his ears and head as the specter began wailing outside the heavy walls. Loud wails pierced the four corners of the house and bounced into their eardrums. It would be a long night as her sobbing eventually quieted into silence, and my family fell fitfully asleep.

It wouldn't be the last time she visited while I was lost. Evil exists and uses our fears to torment us.

My dad saw her and had taken in her form with his own eyes. But it didn't change him. If only it had.

Time never slows, and the days passed by minute by minute until I had lost track of how long Oaxaca had embraced me. My small form had shaped itself in beds under tables and in gardens, shivering as chill winds blew across the empty streets. I slept with my face covered, always covered, so I couldn't see what lay just beyond my view. I was rocked to sleep every night by an unseen hand, and rest found me easily, despite where my body lay.

I found that I could take a shower and sauna in one of the local bathhouses meant only for men. I would slip in and slip out when no one was around and leave clean as a whistle.

I had a friend who worked at a local hotel, and sometimes he let me in late at night to take a swim. As I submerged myself, clad only in underwear, I wondered how my life would have been had I not been lost. Would I have had the chance to make the friends I had and see all the sights I was seeing? I smiled to myself and decided that there was something big I was supposed to accomplish.

I loved the movies and would find a way to

visit the cinema every week. Sometimes I would see a movie three times, always finding the money or slipping in the side door. The theater, to my mind, was grand. I would climb the steps to the balcony with my small plastic bag of soda in one hand and a snack in the other. As I settled into my seat, the room would grow dark and the movie would begin. There would often be a double matinee, and those were my favorite.

One day, I was watching a movie I had already seen several times and was looking forward to the newest feature, which would be played second. Growing slightly bored and knowing every line of the first movie, I squirmed uncomfortably, knowing that I needed to relieve my bladder, but not wanting to go down the steps and into the foyer. I eyeballed the empty bag that had held my soda. I glanced furtively from side to side and realized that there weren't many others on the balcony with me. I opened the bag and let out a big sigh as I took care of business. But what to do with the bag?

I tied it tightly in a knot and sat back in my chair. As my mind churned, I leaned forward on the seat and began to survey the crowd below. People sat happily watching the movie, with a few boys trying to sneak an arm around their girls — and I saw my prey.

I knew the movie by heart, and upcoming was a scene where everybody always jumped and screamed. I waited for the precise minute, and then like a rocket, I sailed that bag of pee through the air to my waiting target. He was trying his awful best to sneak a kiss from the girl he was with, and with a loud splash, the bag nailed him in the head and its contents dripped over him like rain. His girl leaned back in disgust and horror, in sync with the movie screen.

"Puta madre!" he screamed, and looked around, then up, his eyes landing on me grinning over the side of balcony. I dove for the floor, shouts echoing up to me, and made for the stairs and side door, knowing they were coming for me. I sailed through the door just as I could feel the whoosh of shoes behind me, and I disappeared into the streets with a whoop. They couldn't catch me.

On days when I needed to get away from the city, I would cry on the street corners to make some money. The tears came easily, and soon my pockets jingled with the merry tune of gathered coins. I found my friends and said, "Let's go to the lake!" Sometimes they could come and sometimes they had other things to do. We would walk ourselves to the bus station, bags packed with bolillos, cheese, and bananas, and hop on to be transported outside the city.

How did I know how to get places? It seemed I had an innate sense of space and direction and could find the best places to spend the day. Was I born to be self-sufficient? I had been given an overabundance of that, I thought, as we trudged off the bus.

We hiked through the green hills until we came to a small lake. We would swim, splash, and lie on the ground and eat our tortas until we were stuffed. My friends loved to be with me and go on these expeditions because it took them out of their normal routine. Children in those days could go anywhere in Mexico—it wasn't like it is now. Back in the seventies, a bus driver wouldn't blink if a pack of children hopped on.

I felt free and I felt alive, even though a nagging feeling at the back of my neck caused me to pause, wondering about my home and what was going on there. I would watch my friends splashing and having fun, with no worries of their home or families. I thought of my mom, but I remember distinctly the day when her face started to fade from my memory. I could no longer conjure up her long black hair and wide face with high cheekbones smiling at me. This made me sad, and the tears spilled.

Christmas is a magical time in Mexico, with many fiestas and posadas to attend. The posadas are parties held at various places in the streets, houses, and churches of your neighborhood. They begin in the twelve days leading up to Christmas Day. The baby Jesus and his trek to find a place to be born is an important part of Catholic tradition in Mexico.

One person is given the task of dressing a replica of the baby, and when it's time for the posada, neighbors and friends knock on the door and represent the pilgrims, Mary and Joseph, and their quest to find a place for the savior to be born. The house owner shakes his head and says there is no room there. They then carry the baby out the door and file into the street to sing and find a place for him to be born. Many songs are sung, and finally the baby is laid in the manger, at a home prepared for him.

Then the posada begins. Ponche, a hot drink made with many fruits, is served in plastic cups as well as delicious tamales prepared for the occasion. Tamales are made by the hundreds at Christmas time and are a beloved taste and tradition. Pinatas are hung and stuffed with small candies and lots of fruit. If a child from the USA broke a piñata in Mexico, they would be sorely disappointed by the lack of candy, but here the contents are what the kids live for. Oranges, tejocotes, sugar cane, and hard candies tumble out from a brightly covered clay pot that breaks into a million pieces. There is no sharing here, and if you pick up the entire contents yourself then you get to keep it.

I walked down the street and joined a procession, having cleaned myself up and put on the best sweater that I had—but not being able to see myself, I didn't realize it was in tatters and so, so dirty. But my face gleamed, as I had tried to get as much grime off as I could. I was so excited, and with my hands stuffed in my pockets, I excitedly joined the parade that carried the baby Jesus to a posada at the church. My voice sang the songs, and I knew that God loved me. I sang for him and for the baby Jesus, too.

When we arrived, I stood under the bright lights of the courtyard and awaited my turn to hit the piñata. I knew some of the kids at this posada and expected them to smile and hand me the bat when it was my turn. I looked expectantly at them and smiled. The smells of hot punch and tamales made my stomach churn and my mouth salivate. I was so hungry. Sometimes I took communion at the various churches in the city because I was hungry. These fiestas were guarantees that I would eat that evening.

The piñata broke before it was my turn, and I went to grab some of the bounty that had fallen from it. Before I could run into the melee, I felt a hand on my shoulder and turned around to see one of the people who worked at the church looking down into my face. He handed me a cup of punch and one tamale and told me that I had to go—the parents didn't want me there anymore.

I looked around at the happy faces of the kids and the parents milling around talking, and I looked up at him again. "Why do I have to leave?" I uttered in a small voice, my heart sinking slowly to the floor.

"Son, you are so dirty, and we can't have you here."

He took me to the gate and sent me out with a not-so-gentle push from behind. I walked slowly down the street with my finger trailing on the iron fence that surrounded the church and posada contained within. The lights faded as I sat down on the curb some ways away and ate my tamale in darkness. Why didn't they want me there? Those kids were my friends, I thought. Was it because I lived on the streets? Did that make me different from them?

The drink went down sourly to my stomach. I turned in the direction of my bed for the night. I looked inside brightly lit windows as I passed by them, and my greedy eyes saw families around their tables, smiling and laughing with each other, moms and dads who loved their kids and took care of them. Tears fell softly down my cheeks as the last of the tamale settled in my stomach. Why couldn't my mom find me? Did she even care?

Christmas came and went that year, as did

many more days after that, and the streets consumed me.

6.

I have memories of different sets of faces, people and families who wanted to take me in. I like to think that they adopted me and my lonely heart when I was most in need.

I met a family who was visiting Oaxaca for a short getaway. The dad was a bus driver and had driven a tour bus in for a few days, and I happened to be sitting outside the hotel where they were staying.

I was watching the crowd go by, mesmerized by the grandmas with their shawls pulled tightly around their heads, carrying bags filled with bread and tortillas, maybe a chicken leg sticking out. Were they going home to make a delicious lunch for their grandchildren? I cocked my head and pondered them carefully, as a girl a few years older than me sat down on the steps.

"Hola, who are you? Why are you sitting here alone?" she said, with curiosity in her eyes.

I just nodded my head and said, "I live here."

I believe she saw through me, saw the hunger in my eyes, and decided that I would have breakfast with them. When her parents came outside, she introduced me, and we headed to breakfast.

I must have charmed them because when they left for home a few days later, they wanted me to go home with them—to stay. If I went, would I lose all hope of ever being found? Could my mom find me? My head swirled with indecision, but deciding I was tired of sleeping on the concrete, I went with them, not knowing what my fate would be.

They lived in Tehaucán, a town that inched me

a bit closer toward home—though at the time, I didn't know that. I just knew that someone was showing me affection and care, and I had a place to lay my head. The family dynamic in the home was a good one, and the girl who had found me outside the hotel told me once that I was the best brother she had—which only meant that her blood brothers annoyed her, as all brothers will. My heart smiled as I felt something akin to home for the first time in nearly a year. Days and days had gone by without someone to kiss my head goodnight and make me feel safe. I enrolled in school, had a hot meal every night, and wore clothes that weren't in tatters. Yet something seemed amiss to me, and I couldn't quite put my finger on it. Why had they wanted me to live with them?

One day, maybe a month later, a lady stopped me in town as I was walking to school and asked me who I was. "You don't belong to that family. Why are you here?"

A short burst of fear shot through me as I

began to fear she would find me out, that I was an imposter. Her dark eyes pierced me as I fiercely glared back. I knew she could see right through me to who I really was. I didn't belong anywhere.

"Come home with me. I need you to help me at my home. They don't need you; they have lots of children," she said as she grabbed my arm and dragged me down the street.

This is a strange scene—I know it is. But when you are adrift with no anchor, strange things will happen. I had told myself never to become attached to anyone or anything because they would be ripped away from me, like my dad… or my family. I didn't know this lady and I didn't like her, but I felt myself being propelled toward her home on the other side of the city and couldn't seem to stop the forward motion.

I found myself in a small cement home that while not uncomfortable, was not where I wanted to be. Her daughter looked at me as I came in the door and the woman told her that I would be staying with them. The daughter was nice, at first, as was the mom. The dad came and went, always busy with work and not connecting with the dynamic of this family. I was immediately put to work cleaning, working outside, and doing lots of labor.

The daughter would sit inside with her boyfriend while the mom was at work, and they would kiss and make out while she weirdly looked at me over his shoulder. I believe she wanted me to see them and what they were doing. "Go do my dishes for me, Toño," she would say as she ran her finger down the side of her boyfriend's face. "I don't want to do them." And she would look away and open her mouth to take in his tongue and seemingly swallow it.

Her boyfriend looked at me and shouted, "You heard her! Get out of here and do her dishes!" His slicked-back hair was greasy with pomade and made me want to puke. I ran out the door to the stack of dishes sitting in the concrete sink, and I began to wash.

It seems that the family who had brought me

to Tehaucán was looking for me, and they found me. They proceeded to get into a nasty argument with the lady who had taken me off the street.

"He is ours. He's been living with us after we found him in Oaxaca," the first family argued.

"But you have many children, you don't need him. I need him here to help us," said the second lady. "Besides, we've filed to adopt him."

Anger flashed in the first mom's eyes as she disputed that fact with her own in-process court documents. "That is a lie—we are adopting him, and here is the proof."

I felt myself go out of my body, like Kaliman, and wished I could transport my soul back to the little white house and be with my mom. I didn't care about my stepdad; I could try to avoid him. I just wanted to go home—not stay with these families who were fighting over someone that wasn't even theirs in the first place.

After much arguing, I did go home with the first family. My head felt large and too big for my body as I entered the house and lay down on my bed.

Two months had passed since I left Oaxaca, in a series of days and weeks and now years that had begun to blur in my mind. I saw that they were serious about keeping me with them, and the unease I felt didn't leave me.

The next day, a visiting nurse they had arranged for arrived at the house with inoculations to administer to me. She pulled out a huge needle that shone menacing in the small light hanging from the ceiling. I took one look at that needle and ran out the door and boarded a train back to Oaxaca. I remembered the train station when I had come though there, and I rode the rails right back to those hard streets they'd plucked me from. I left with nothing, and I never saw them again.

Does this story seem abrupt to you? My life was a series of comings, goings, and leavings, in unison with the promise I had made myself not to become attached to anyone. Little strands of hardness had begun to grow around my heart, and all I could do was make them stronger—so strong that they couldn't be broken. Distrust ruled me, yet my life on the streets seemed a better choice than being in someone's home who was using me for their own gain. I would never belong to someone else.

The Oaxacan sun shone hot and heavy on the zocalo in town as I sat under the shade of a tree. Save for the middle of the night, this town never seemed to slow down, and a steady influx of tourists was always appearing. Oaxaca was slowly beginning to be noticed by people outside of Mexico, so there was a never a shortage of different faces to be seen.

Along with that were the hustlers of the city, me included. My boys and I learned to mess with the tourists and distract them while the other one snuck a wallet out of a pocket or jewelry from a wrist. They never noticed the weight of it disappearing as my charm exuded a spell over them. I would sing a song or do a little dance to keep them watching me, and when they had handed over a few coins and a smile, I slipped away, waving as I went. I became as good as you can get, while learning to survive. I reasoned that if I kept giving at least half of what I earned to the church, that God would forgive me for the stealing. It was a rush that became a part of my everyday life, as sure as breathing.

These facts didn't take away from who I was, who I knew I was born to be. I knew I had a purpose that I needed to find, and being lost wasn't helping me get there.

One day, an older girl that I was friends with came to find me. "There is a man who will pay you to come with him," she said. "He will pay you good." I looked at her carefully and asked why he wanted me to come with him. "He's just over there." She pointed to a white man wearing a hat. "He told me he wanted you, and only you, to come with him. He said he'll pay me good as well if you go with him."

I looked at the man, and my mouth turned sour. He was sitting there, cocksure of himself and the fact that he felt he could do what he wanted, and I looked at her and shook my head no. It didn't feel right, and as she walked over to him and let him know, he glanced over with a dark look on his face. It was quickly replaced with a slick smile as he got up to approach me.

I turned and ran down the street before he could reach me. There were many so-called "tourists" who came here, came looking for sex with children. Several of my friends had succumbed to the lure of money and were never the same afterward. Privilege, at its lurid worst, believes it can take advantage of poverty, and I knew I couldn't do much to change that fact. I would come to see an even darker side to these truths.

Days and nights blurred together in a succession of hazy dreams, stitched together by the fabric of daylight. At night, I huddled under my newspapers. Other times, I was lucky enough to lay my head on the chair of a hotel patio, the pool beside it reflecting my face in the moonlight.

It was a charade, really, a sham of what my life was. People lived their lives and went on vacation to a place such as Oaxaca, without cares or thoughts of the faces they passed in the crowd. A simple thing like a pool was an expected thing, a place to sit down and dip your toes. No thoughts were given to a small boy, somewhere between seven and eight years old, who laid his head down at night and gazed at the waters, a boy whose dreams of his old life were just beyond his grasp. When you have tangible things, you come to expect a certain way of life.

I never took what I had for granted. Each piece of sweet bread I dipped in a bowl of hot chocolate was an experience to be savored. Each leftover sandwich I retrieved from a plate at the tourist restaurants I ate with dignity and a napkin to wipe the mayo off the corner of my mouth. I kept myself straight and erect, never doubting my worth in the world.

Moments would come, though, when my defenses were down, and I had a recurring dream—a dream where I let myself imagine things that could never happen. My mouth would become dry and my body would shudder as the dream tore through me. In my dream I was huddled on the street corner crying, and all the kids who were my friends surrounded me laughing and saying that I had no mom, no family. "You're all alone! You have nobody!" their voices would hiss. Fingers pointed at me and faces twisted like demons would come to torment me to the point of exhaustion. I didn't want to spend one more night on the street. Then from up above, I could hear a whirring which turned into a loud roar, and in front of me on the street, a helicopter landed. The door opened, and out of the helicopter stepped my mom who began slowly moving toward me with her arms open, saying, "Hijo! I've been looking for you! Where have you been?" In my dream I would run to her arms and bury myself in her chest. We would climb into the chopper and I would look out and wave goodbye to my friends who had tormented me, their look of confusion enough satisfaction for me. And we would fly home.

I dreamed this dream at night, and sometimes in daydreams languid as a hazy summer day. The unquenched ache took over my entire being, and the burning of that dream still haunts me.

Christmas, a time of joy and wonder in most children's lives, had arrived yet again in Oaxaca. Festive lights were strung across the streets, and indigenous people arrived with their very colorful and resplendent crafts and wares. Their crinkled, warm faces smiled, and the sugary treats they made were piled up and presented in huge baskets to be consumed with gusto. Nothing was more comforting when it slid down your throat. Tamales, hot and steamy, nestled in their husks of corn, awaited hands to break apart and taste them. Tamales are Christmas.

Though the sights and sounds were exciting to see, I realized it would be the third Christmas away from my family. I imagined them setting up the manger scene, with its elaborate moss and rocks, tucked under branches hanging with shiny lights and balls. My mom, with her long hair hanging in a single braid down her back, would be stirring the tamale mixture with her hand, as she has done a thousand times before. My brother would be outside playing with friends and would know he had a house to come home to when the afternoon light faded into dusk.

For me, Christmas was going to be just another day, and I decided that I wouldn't celebrate it. But life and its minutes have other things in mind, and a family that I knew from around town asked me if I wanted to come and live with them for a while. I was tired, so tired of running and fending for myself that I gave in and said yes.

Their home was a small but clean adobe house away from the square. It was a humble abode, and they had some animals plus a small barn out back.

In the weeks leading up to Christmas, I stayed with them and helped them in the home. My bed was made up in the small barn, so every night I lay on my mat and could hear the animals nickering softly as if to tell me, "It's okay, Toño, everything will be all right." I took comfort in those small moments as I laid down my head each evening.

Preparations for Navidad were under way hot and heavy in the streets, and I saw people hurrying with bags filled with treats and small gifts for their loved ones. A pang dropped inside me as I realized that I had never received a Christmas gift—not even in the years living at home. My mom came from such a small Indian village that gifts were not something that were highly valued. Maybe a good meal and celebration was called for, but money spent on frivolous things was not something that was done.

On Christmas Eve, after the last tamale was eaten and we laid our heads down to sleep, I closed my eyes and whispered, "God, I know you are with me, but can you show me that I'm going to be okay? That you haven't left me alone forever?"

I drifted off into a thoroughly deep and dreamless sleep that left me awakening with the first rooster crowing. I could hear the animals moving slowly in their pens, telling me to wake up and greet the day. My thoughts once again drifted back to my family, and as I sat up and ran my fingers through my hair, I noticed a small package wrapped in stiff brown paper and tied with a red string. A surge of hope crested through me as I carefully picked it up and turned it over.

It can't be for me, I thought, but there it was—my name in bold letters: T-O-N-O.

I tore gently at the edges until the paper was very neatly unwrapped, and there nestled inside was a blue shirt. A simple shirt, really, with three buttons at the top and a collar to match.

My eyes filled with hot tears and I knew God hadn't forgotten me in my sadness. For the first time in a very long while, I felt hope—hope that I would get home and that there was a purpose for me. I peeled off my dirty shirt from the night before and slipped on the blue one. It shone clean and sparkly against my dark hair and eyes that had nearly been stripped of hope. I stepped outside the barn to embrace the light of the Christmas morning.

7.

Behind the scenes of every story, just beyond the edges of where reality lies, is someone working hard to make sure the tale has an ending—good or bad. The story must go on, and my story is just a blip on the radar of the past, a small indentation that didn't make a lot of waves. I was one small boy thrust on a world that I didn't comprehend, a boy who missed home.

Tossed and thrown, I wasn't given much hope of survival by any of my family who knew I was missing. Moms, though, never give up, even when the darkest of night presses in on them. Even when their husband tells them they can't look for their own child. Even then, they will say that they feel something, that their kids are not gone or dead, as that reality must come when a child is gone for that long.

That "something" was working hard to make right what had been wrong for so long; and somewhere along the line, on a side street of Oaxaca, Mexico, a little magic happened.

I had an aunt, Tia Augustina, my mom's sister, who lived in Oaxaca. She didn't live in town, and I don't remember much about her. I'm sure I would have met her when I was small, but today—or then—I couldn't picture her face if I tried. I now know she lived in a village outside the city limits and made treks into the city several times a month. The mercados in the city had much to offer, as well as a time to get out of the house and see something new.

My tia had a friend who lived in the city, and that friend was a regular on the streets I inhabited.

Fate, or destiny, happened one morning when she saw me running around the market, clothes semi-tattered but black hair shining as I ran. I may never know what caused her to look at me in a different way—not just a nuisance running around in the market creating chaos—but she did. My nose, very Aztec in shape and form, was recognizable, and she studied me carefully as I disappeared from her sight.

"Who was that boy?" she asked one of the vendors as he wrapped up her meat in a brown paper package.

"He's one of the local boys. I don't know; he's just always around," said the butcher as she handed him several pesos to cover her purchase.

Her mind started churning, and when she got home, she made it a point to decide on a day to visit her friend, my Tia Augustina. Not many people in rural Mexico had phones in late summer of 1976, so to talk to my aunt, she needed to make time to take a bus to my tia's village and walk up several dusty side streets to find Augustina's casita.

She found my aunt outside, washing up the dishes from the morning, and greeted her with a kiss on both cheeks. "Hola, comadre, how are you this morning?" she said heartily, as my aunt smiled in welcome.

"Pasale, pasale! Come in!" my tia said. "What brings you here?"

As they completed the niceties of Mexican properness—small talk, coffee, sweet bread, and the offer of a meal—it finally came round to the reason for the visit. "Comadre, doesn't your sister have a boy who's been missing for several years?" she mused. "He would be around nine or ten years old?"

My tia's eyes took on a faraway look as she thought about that question—thought about me.

"Yes, she does. He's been gone for three years now, and Eva has nearly given up," my tia said wearily. "Pobrecita. Her husband doesn't even let her look for him."

Her friend clucked her tongue and shook her

head, then looked her in the eye and said a few words that changed the direction of my life. "Augustina, there is a boy that I saw in the market. He looks like the description that you told me about years ago," she said with concern in her eyes. "He looks like Toño."

My aunt sat quietly, sifting through the thoughts in her mind. She turned her face toward the window and got out pen and paper and had her friend write a letter to my mom. When my aunt's friend left the house that day, she was holding a letter, holding the information that would change my mom's life. As the letter dropped into the post office slot, the earth shifted slightly on its axis.

My mom, going about her day-to-day life, was unaware of what was transpiring. In my absence, she and my stepdad had added Lourdes to the family with more soon to follow. Life had gone on without me, and my stepdad was happy, as happy as his alcoholic mind would let him be. He had his woman and children who were his and his alone.

His mind was a furtive, dark place that held no room for what was not his—a reminder that she had been with another man. But an abusive soul doesn't rest unless it is creating madness, and my mom suffered greatly under his hand. She put from her mind the pain of her past: my dad, her dead babies, and me, who was lost to her. When you suffer trauma, you begin to separate events in your mind, or set them aside only to bring out when your brain allows it. Did her husband exist? Was he murdered or had he committed suicide? Did she have other babies and a son who disappeared? She set those moments, those memories aside because she had to. She couldn't mention the name *Antonio* in front of her husband—for he was her husband now—or the rage would begin.

But fate had other plans, and one day a man came rapping on the fence that surrounded the little white house. She was home alone with the baby while Chucho was at school. The man held a letter in his hand and passed it to her through the gate.

"What is this?" she asked the mail carrier as she looked at it in her hands.

"Are you Doña Evangelina Bautista Hernandez?" he asked, looking through the gate at the letter.

"I am," she said.

He smiled and kept walking with his bike. "Then the letter is for you."

She puzzled a bit, wondering who could have sent her a letter, but didn't open it. Her girlhood had not included school nor the craft of reading and writing. She spoke two languages, but the written word was not something she had learned. Lourdes scrambled around her feet, and she went inside and laid the letter on the table until Chucho came home. He could read it to her.

My brother and mom sat at the table with smoke from the fire outside drifting lazily in spirals around them. Beans were set low on a metal grill on top of the flames, and they bubbled merrily, emitting a delicious fragrance. It went unnoticed, though, as the words Chucho was reading began to slowly sink in.

"Ma, Toño is alive! He's alive! I know it!" he shouted, causing his little sister to cry at the tone of his voice. "It has to be him! We have to go, Ma!"

My mom sat stock still, with tears rolling down her face. Could something so longed-for, so hidden inside her heart become truth? And just then, a shadow darkened the door and my stepdad walked in, drunk and reeking of whatever he had imbibed that day.

"Que paso!" he shouted, stumbling over to the table and taking a hard seat. "Why are you crying, chinga?"

She looked up at him and then looked away, afraid of his response when she would tell him what her sister had sent them, the information contained therein. She didn't have to speak because Chucho could hold it in no longer.

"Tia Augustina sent us a letter. Her friend believes she saw Toño in Oaxaca!" My brother's voice broke as he implored his dad to believe, to accept, and to not get angry.

My stepdad looked blearily at him, with flashes of something deep in his eyes. "Let me see that letter. I don't believe this is true. It's not him." He scanned it quickly and threw it on the table, then stumbled to the bed and fell into it. Soon, his violent snores and the stench of alcohol were permeating the room.

Chucho looked at my mom, who was still crying in the chair. "Ma, you have to go. You have to go see if it's him." The urgency in his voice broke her out of her reverie, and she stood up and set the baby on the floor.

There was no money, there was never any money because her husband drank it away before it made it into her hands. My mom knew she would need to borrow money to get to Oaxaca to find me, so she went to the neighbor who held the money in the tanda—a pool of saved money— neighborhood women give to in small amounts each week. When a nice amount is raised, they give the money to someone in the group who needs it, and they start over again. This time, it was my mom's turn. Money in hand, she went home and hid it because with an alcoholic, no money is safe.

She served the comida, with my stepdad still passed out on the bed and later put the kids to sleep. She lay down beside him and went to sleep.

In the morning, as the coffee was brewing briskly in a pot, she told my stepdad she was going to Oaxaca to bring Toño home.

"You don't even know if it's him," he said, a shadow crossing his face, one she knew well.

"I'm going," she said. "I have to know if it's him."

She could feel the air pass before her face before his hand struck, hard and swift, across her head. She stumbled backwards as he came at her with rage in his eyes,

"Am I not enough? Are your kids not enough? He is not my son!"

His fist connected with her smooth, brown cheekbones, and the crunch of the blow sent an electric jolt straight through to her brain as she landed hard against the wall and slid to the floor. Blood, in a tiny spiral, trickled down her cheek and fell onto the floor. As he turned to leave, his heavy boot smeared the drop of blood, and he left spots as he walked out the door to find his next drink.

She sat up heavily, Lourdes crying loudly, and told Chucho to pack a few things. "You're staying with the neighbors for a few days so I can go to Oaxaca. I need to know if it's him," she said painfully as she touched her face. They raced around the house, she deposited the kids safely down the street with a neighbor, and she boarded a train heading south.

Women didn't travel alone much in Mexico at that time, but the situation was dire, and she was a mom trying to find her child. The train chugged south into the familiar, lush landscape she had been born into. It had been three years since they left here, and she missed it. *Could my Toño be here? How could he have come here alone?* Thoughts bubbled in her mind like so many fragments, pieces that have no home.

She arrived at the train station and found a bus to her sister's home outside the city. They chatted deep into the night, deciding what was the best way to approach this. Then they went to sleep to dream of what the next day would hold.

Me? After a hot day, I was holding onto what little I had and was bedding down for the night under the table that had often sheltered me. I pulled the newspapers tight over my body and curled up in a ball to fall asleep.

The next morning rose hot and bright, like so many days did. I ambled around the zocalo, finding bits and pieces of bread and leftover eggs to get me by. I went by the market to see if my friends were around, but school had started and they were nowhere to be found. It was days like this that I longed to go to school and study. My brain was itching to learn, and I was tired of trudging the streets with no goal in mind.

The afternoon sun was wearing thin as I sat down on the street corner to perform my trick— my crying game. The streets were busy, and I put my head down with my hands over my eyes. Several people tossed me coins, but the cement felt cool underneath me and I kept my head down so I could rest it.

Out of the corner of my eye, I saw a lady walking slowly down the street. She looked at me intently, as if searching my small frame for signs of recognition in the shape of my back or the curve of my face. I peered at her hesitantly. Something familiar about her struck me, and I lifted my head to look at her as she came closer.

"Toño?" she said softly, with hope in her eyes. I stood up, and suddenly her face came into view—her dark eyes, the shape of her face, the long black braid.

"Ma?" I said.

She ran toward me and I ran toward her and we met in a violent embrace. I melted downward,

downward as I sunk into her arms.

"Where have you been?" she cried, as her river of tears spread slowly onto my parched skin. She was here; I was with her. The hardness of my heart melted as I stared into her face.

We stayed at my tia's house for a day, then wasted no time in boarding the train to Maquixco where my brother awaited my return. My mom and I sat together, silently, she holding onto me like a newborn babe returned to the breast. It would be a pattern that repeated itself for decades.

I laid my head on her shoulder and slept. For the first time in three years I didn't have to stay aware, on guard. I wasn't sure what awaited me. My mind walked through different scenarios, pictures of my brother, and memories of the house. My stepdad? I tried not to think of him, but I knew I had to face him. I had changed, though, in my time gone. Three years of being self-sufficient does something to you; it changes you until you almost don't recognize yourself. For me, it was a good change. Even though I was only nine years old, I had lived a lot in those lost years.

My spine stiffened just a bit, and I vowed that I wouldn't let him hurt me anymore. And the train headed north.

8.

A breeze blew on our faces as we headed down the small lane that led to the white house. My heart beat out of my chest, and I couldn't believe I was here. I could hear the echo of my brother's voice call back to me as I dawdled on the way to school that morning three years past— would my life have been better if I had listened? Oaxaca flashed in my mind, and I pondered whether I could have found my way home. Maybe, I don't know. I hadn't really known where home was, but Oaxaca had become my home in the spaces of time that I had spent there, in the verdant zocalo where I ran freely with my friends and in the markets where kind faces fed me a bit of bread or drink nearly every day.

As we approached the house, apprehension overcame me until my brother Chucho came tearing out of the neighbor's yard.

"Toño! Toño!" he shouted, tearing around the corner to grab me and hug me hard. I held onto him, always knowing that he had never given up hope for me.

A small little girl was brought out by the neighbor, and my mom introduced me to my sister and brother. I hesitated, thinking about my sister and brother who had died soon after my dad. The little girl looked at me with a sober look on her face, then gently reached out to touch me and giggled. I smiled, and the spell of the past was broken.

My mom was happy and smiling, and this was how I could still remember her, but deeper down I could see a sadness that had mixed into her very soul. Was it because of me?

A black head full of wavy hair and a face with a large moustache was waiting just inside the gate of the white house. His eyes pierced me as we walked through. I felt small, yet big, as if I knew he could never hurt me again. Shadows followed him, and he walked up to us, no smile on his face or welcome for my mom. He knew how much she had wanted me back, and he knew he had stopped her from looking for me.

He looked me up and down, and I could see a small drop of spittle hanging on his lip. He opened his mouth, and with all the things he ever did to me and would do, these were the words I would remember him saying: "I thought you were dead."

I believe my path to leaving home again was being paved that day. I didn't yet know it, but as the days passed, with a startling clarity I saw the heaviness that hung over our house.

My dad was not the patriarch he thought he

was. Lourdes toddled around outside in a yard devoid of color, with another baby soon to come. My mom worked hard, so hard, to keep food on the table as he tipped back and drank the miniscule amount of money he earned doing cement work. He wasn't a forward thinker and never would be. While people were digging pipes and bringing in running water, my mom still filled basin after basin of water to boil for drinking as well as bathing. We had no toilet, no shower, and no heater to warm us in the colder months. The Mexican people are a proud culture that prides itself on moving forward yet holding onto the past with integrity and a serving of chicken and mole. In other words, we don't stay still—we progress and make ourselves new. My stepdad, though, didn't believe in this. Any change would threaten his control and the way he ruled his roost. He was indicative of a patriarchal culture that was dying a slow death, but he was hanging onto it with all his might. It turns out he would never relinquish that control. Ever.

Sleeping on the floor had become the norm for me, but every night our entire family slept on petates. Sore by morning, my mom never complained. We should have beds, I thought, and quickly thought of ways we could get them. What can I do or sell?

But my plans would crash around me when he would stumble in, inebriated and cursing, and she would get up quickly and start to heat his supper that he had missed hours ago. She didn't chide him or ask him where he was, and the room was permeated with the stink of him. I glared at him from where I sat, and he looked at me, slurring every word out of his mouth. "What are you looking at? Why did you even bother making your mom come look for you? You're nothing but trouble to me." And the words hit me, like a thrown stone, as he fell onto the floor to begin his house-razing snores.

"Ma," I said, whispering urgently to her. "Why do you stay here? Let's go! There are better places to live!"

Her eyes would look at me softly as she glanced over at the baby making a gleeful mess of her food on the table. There was that smile again—the smile that said, *I will never leave. There's nothing out there for me.* Each time I saw my mom do this a little piece of my heart hardened once more.

I began school once again and tried to connect with the friends I had left behind when I was lost. Once when I was walking down our lane, I saw a small boy about my age being bullied by a gang of kids. His back was bent and misshapen, a large hump extending upward behind his neck. I recognized my friend Chon, and I chased the other boys away. Chon became a solace for me, and we spent many hours together, riding back and forth on the lane with his donkey. We pretended I was the Lone Ranger and he was Tonto, riding our wild steed into danger to rescue the damsel in distress. When we got hungry, he would pull out of his pockets smashed, crusty rolls smeared with beans. I would laugh, and he would tear them in half to share. Chon was one of the best friends I've ever had, and his appearance was part of who he was. We played the Hunchback of Notre Dame as well, and he had a starring role in that fantasy. He was a good friend and loved me for me. The time I spent with him, each minute, was a balm for my soul. He didn't ask questions but simply existed in each moment.

I had a teacher at the school that I loved. Her name was Adelita, and she was the first person to really fight for me. She took to me from the very first day and became the advocate I never had. We all had a crush on her as she was beautiful, and she cared about what happened to me.

Though I could be naughty and tease the girls, everyone liked me. I got good grades and quickly came up to speed from time lost on the streets. Still, I would appear at school with bruises and cuts on my face and neck, and Adelita would ask me what happened. I always told her I fell or that

I had a bike accident—just so I didn't have to tell her the truth. I was ashamed by my home and the way my family lived. I wanted more for them, and my teacher wanted more for me.

"Who is hurting you?" she would ask me, concern flitting through her eyes. "I want to meet your family and your dad in particular."

"He's not my dad," I quickly retorted. "He's my stepdad."

"Well, I need to talk to him. I want to see him face-to-face," she answered, gathering me after school one day to take me home in the pouring rain. We climbed into her groovy VW Beetle and buzzed in the direction of my house. I didn't want her to see it, and I didn't want her to meet my dad, yet admiration filled me as we got out and she boldly knocked on the door.

My dad sidled up and open the door slowly.

"Are you Antonio's stepfather?" she asked.

"Yes, I'm Rutilio Jimenez," he said smoothly, a look of anger smoldering in his eyes. "Why do you ask?" He looked down at me and wordlessly conveyed his feelings.

"I want to tell you that your son is an amazing student. He is very smart and has learned so much in the time he's come back. He has surpassed the grade he's in, and we want to move him forward."

He threw his head back and laughed, as the pulque he had drunk started working on him. "You must be mistaken," he said. "You can't mean him. He's not smart at all." My face burned hot, and I looked anywhere but his face, where I could see he was struggling with her words.

"No," she said. "I do mean Antonio. He is a wonderful student, and I wanted to make sure that you knew that."

He looked at her with eyes as cold as a glass full of ice and spat, "You mean you came all the way over here in that little car with him to tell me that?"

She nodded and stuck out her hand to shake his firmly. "Thank you for hearing me." Looking down at me, she said, "I'll see you tomorrow." With that, she turned on her heel and smartly walked back to her Bug and drove off.

I felt a sharp pain in my ear as he grabbed it between his fingernails and dragged me inside. I knew that he was embarrassed, and I knew that I was the reason. I looked at him defiantly.

"Why would you bring your snotty bitch of a teacher over here to make me look bad? To make me look like I don't know anything?"

I saw his fist coming and dodged it deftly before I ran outside and down the lane. I could hear his voice yelling loudly behind, shouting, "You can't run forever!"

Most of the times when incidents like this happened, he left and got so drunk that he didn't remember what he had said or done. I could stay away just long enough and slip back in just in time for some food and to head to bed. What I wondered then, and even now, is where my mom was. Why didn't she defend me? I knew he would beat her just as hard and long as me, but not even a "please stop" came from her lips. I loved her so much and knew she didn't deserve to be with someone as awful as him.

In addition to my teacher at school, my brother and I had a coach who recognized in us our ability to run track. We were still in elementary, but he put us in races together and we were unstoppable. We didn't have money for running shoes, so we ran barefoot! My stepdad, although a sports fan, didn't want us to do anything that involved money.

When we had won medals in our area enough to advance to a race in Mexico City, the coach came to our house to talk to him.

"They are very good," he said. "We need your permission for them to race outside our area. Will you let us have it?"

My dad struggled for words and said he wouldn't give any money toward it. "I know that Chucho can run, but Toño should stay here," he said. The words hit me like a stinging rain.

"No," said the coach, "they're better together, and I need them both."

My stepdad's face clouded over; someone had

usurped his authority once again.

We did race in Mexico City, and we brought home a medal for it. Our coach had paid for our passage and meals for the day out of his own pocket, but he had said it was worth it for how well we had done. We had made him proud, he said.

When we arrived back home, my stepdad praised Chucho for his ability, and I went and hid my medal underneath my clothes, to be brought out when I alone could look at it.

We were dirt poor, and I didn't like it. My mind was always spinning with ideas to make money and become a better me. My mom would sometimes sell soda to tourists to make money. My brother and some of my friends decided to start selling popsicles to tourists as well.

I pleaded with my mom. "Ma, just give me ten pesos, and I'll bring you one hundred pesos back."

"What do you need ten pesos for? That's a lot," she mused as she fished her coin purse out of her blouse. Money in hand, I hugged her and ran off with Chucho, my cousin Gorio, and my friend Juan. We headed toward the pyramids and the gold mine that was to be found there.

We lived one mile from the ancient pyramids that sit majestically in Teotihuacán. The Pyramid of the Sun and the Pyramid of the Moon anchor an ancient city that is mostly uncovered, but with more being discovered and unearthed day by day. Tourists flock from all over the world, as well as Mexico, to behold the wonder of the pyramids. My mom, at times, had sold different things in the Avenue of the Dead, the road that leads in between the pyramids and holds many vendors.

Tall, with crumbly steps, the pyramids sit in the sun's heavy path, and by the time the people reach the base of the steps, they are heavy with sweat. We purchased our boxes of popsicles and started selling. We would race up the side of the pyramids—in the cordoned off areas where no one was supposed to go—and reach the sweaty masses as they reached the top. It was a way to make money, and I was good at it. As before, my charm and quick wit was a favorite with the tourists, and I sold out of popsicles before they could even begin to melt. I bought more and more boxes until my pockets were lined with coins.

At the end of each day, I would give my mom part of the money I made and would bury the rest in the dirt where only I could find it. My dad would shout, "Where are you getting this money? You can't be making that much selling popsicles to the people!" I ran from him before he could catch me and take the money from me. Many months in the future, I would only be able to take some of the money I had hidden, as I left in a hurry. I believe to this day I still have money buried in Mexico.

My cousin Gregorio—Gorio for short—was my favorite cousin. I loved him like a brother and spent many days in his home with his brothers and sisters as well as his mom, who loved me like her own. I had known, or rather felt, that God was with me when I was lost, and I reasoned that he would stay with me if I wanted him to. I asked my aunt lots of questions. They were Jehovah's Witnesses, who, although they believe in Jesus as the Christ, do not believe in the Trinity, which is sacred to the way I grew up. She told me many tales of Jehovah, and I listened raptly as she spun story after story from the Bible. She gave me a hug and said, "Toño, I wish you were my son."

When I got home and we were eating around the table, I told my mom and stepdad about my aunt and how she had taught me about Jehovah. Before the word could even settle in the air, my face was transported sideways by a slap so hard I could feel my teeth rattle.

"I never want to hear that word again in this house," he said, setting my body on edge. "His name is not Jehovah. Never say that word again." My head spun and my cheek stung a hard red where his fingers had touched me. I glared at my stepdad darkly as he stuffed food in his mouth, never looking back at me.

My mom was there, but she wasn't. She was filled with days of taking care of the home and managing a life with an alcoholic husband who hit her whenever the mood would strike. It was a slim piece of day when she didn't get up fast enough to heat up his meal or she didn't turn to answer him properly. Or if I ate too much food or became a nuisance in his line of vision, she would get the blame for me, especially me, as well. Blood and fists and blows to the head—we each experienced enough random violence that the days looked bleak.

And so, she fell silent and decided to ship me off to live with my Uncle Alvaro in Mexico City for a short time.

My uncle was much younger than my mom, and he always pushed to make himself better, to do well in life. He was married, and at the time I lived with them, they didn't have kids. My grandpa, my mom's dad, lived near them and had remarried a nice woman long after my grandma died when my mom was small. I never had known my grandma. But my tia who was married to Alvaro was a woman of rules, and though she could be hard to get along with, she wasn't unkind.

I would follow Alvaro to work most days, as he was a painter and worked for himself. I would watch him dip the brush into the paint and follow his strokes as the wall came to life under his hands. I was mesmerized by the transformation and began to help him as well, and he praised me for my skill. I learned how to wash and take care of your tools, as well as talk to and deal with customers when a job started and finished. I learned from him how to be kind and pleasant when you're working and how to better yourself every day to become the best you can be.

He would take me to the lucha libre every week, and we would watch the wrestlers fly through the air and land on top of one another with ease. The Mexican wrestlers were amazing in their ability to entertain—and I became a big fan of Blue Demon, Mil Mascaras, and especially El Santo. We went to the cinema as well and saw Charles Bronson brood on screen while my uncle and I sat in suspense.

My aunt, though, seemed to be jealous of our time spent together and didn't let me go with him every day like I wanted. Some days I would spend with my step-grandma, who cleaned houses for the rich people in Mexico City. She was kind and she loved me. We would go to houses and I would stare in wonder at the massive structures that had pools blue as a cool drink that glistened on their back patios. Sometimes my grandma would make me a sandwich in their kitchens with the refrigerators I had never seen before humming in the corner. *Why don't we have these?* I told myself I would have it all when I got older. I would never live the way my stepdad lived. He wanted the past, while I wanted the future.

I wasn't in Mexico City for more than a month

when my aunt decided to send me home. We hadn't gotten along the greatest—why, I'll never know—but I arrived back at the white house once again. Simmering there, just below the surface, was a boiling pot ready to explode.

9.

I could have taken the beatings if I would have known why he thought I deserved them. I began to feel separated from my mom just enough to see and wonder why she couldn't leave him. I would later come to realize an abuser has the abused under his control—and my stepdad hated me because he couldn't control me.

Little things caused him to snap, like a cup on the floor or a sidelong look he'd think I had given him. There was really no reason why he acted the way he did unless the demon of alcohol stood up and took the blame. I blamed him, though. Every single fist that connected with bone was his fault. Every drop of blood that fell on the floor. It was all him, even if he never could admit what he did was wrong. If you cross an abusive personality with a glass of pulque, what you get is a bomb ready to go off at all hours, all minutes. My mom and my brother walked on eggshells around him, and the babies were too small to take note. But not me, never me. I would look him in the eye until he had to turn away, and that made him even angrier. I knew it was coming to a head; I just didn't know when.

School continued, and I was enjoying my classes because school took me away from home and the confusing feelings I felt when I was there. Any time I could be away was a good day. I was excelling in school and studied hard so my teacher would be proud of me. Some days I wanted to quit school only because I yearned to seek more, as I had been on my own for so long. My stepdad said I'd need to work. He tried to get me to go to work with him, hard manual labor, but I refused. I didn't want to learn the drudge work and would have chosen a beating before falling into that pattern. So I stayed in school.

Chucho and I would walk home in comfortable silence, kicking rocks and picking up insects to thoughtfully inspect. I loved him, and right then he was the only good thing in my life. We never talked about why my stepdad did the things he did. It was an unspoken thing that the monkey in the room was to be ignored. We played futbol, ran in the streets with friends, and never talked about the abuse that happened to me at home. Chucho did not get the same treatment as I did, though he did suffer at our dad's hand at times. The younger ones and the ones to come would never know or realize the trauma we had suffered. They would never believe it.

When we arrived home from school one day, he was waiting at the gate. His eyes were dark with drink, his frame lazy and lolling as he yelled up the lane.

"Get in here right now," he spoke under his

breath but loud enough to hear. People looked away as we passed by for they knew, everyone knew, that Rutilio Jimenez was not a nice man.

We arrived at the gate, and he grabbed me by the ear and dragged me inside.

"Why do you make a fool of me?" he slurred. "I've done everything for you, but you make me a fool by even looking at me."

I looked at Chucho and back at him, trying to make sense of what he was trying to say. But it didn't matter. "Did you buy my Faros?" he shouted, as I tried to remember him asking me to get the little package of strong cigarettes.

"No," I said. "I didn't."

I could feel Chucho flinch, and my mom let out a little scream as my body careened back against the hard adobe of the house. My head smacked the wall and my sight dimmed before I found my footing and stood upright. I looked straight into his eyes, and as I did, he grabbed me with a vengeance and hauled me into the small barn we had behind the house. My neck felt ready to snap from the pressure he was exerting, and I could half see Chucho running behind me with a look on his face I'll never forget.

He threw me inside, came in, and locked the door. I heard banging and shouting outside. "Take off your clothes," he said, as his putrid breath washed over my face. It smelled of days spent on the sidewalk, sleeping off a drunk.

I glared back at him, and his eyes held fury as his fist connected on my cheekbones with a startling crack. I fell back, and for a moment, I lay feeling the bones in my face slide sideways as I put my hands beside me and let the cool floor center me. I would not cry. I stood up and looked back at him once again, and I closed my eyes as the blows rained down on me.

Dimly, through the haze of pain, I could hear my mom and my brother outside the door, speaking words I couldn't grasp, couldn't comprehend. My mom must have had a key, and she was inside before I could stop her. I didn't want her to get hurt, but he saw her before I could tell her to go back. With his giant uppercut, she fell to the floor, head bouncing like a bouncy ball against the hard-packed dirt. Ruby splashes sprayed the walls and dripped in silent protest to the shame it was witnessing.

Chucho slipped in and drug her out by the armpits, and he glanced at me helplessly as my stepdad locked the door once again. It was him and I—as it always had been. His hatred for me was unquenched and full of a fury born from an endless sea of alcohol and jealousy.

He cocked his head and circled the room as he decided what would come next. His moustache wide across his face, dark fantasies he had held played a game in his brain, telling him to carry them out, to punish me for being born. I could see his gears turning and knew the hate he harbored was because of my dad, the only one who ever really loved me because I was his, blood and flesh stretched over a frame of his making. Sex meant possession to my stepdad, and my mom had slept with another man and bore him not one child but three.

The blackness in him reached the top of his skull as he kicked my side with his dusty, worn boots. Boots that had never done anything good for anyone. I couldn't breathe, and the warm redness coming from my mouth was not from a cut anywhere on my face—it was coming from within. My naked body lay in a ball on the floor, curled in on itself, and I willed the tears not to come. He would never see them. Never.

He hauled me up, and I could see the last rays of the day filtering softly through the slats of the door. People finished their last chores and filed into their homes for dinner as my brokenness was placed on my feet in the middle of the barn. He reached for two bricks laying in the corner and came to stand directly in front of me.

"Sabes que? You are nothing. You will never be anything," he said so softly that I could barely hear him. I looked coldly at him and stood as straight as I could manage. "Hold out your arms," he uttered. My arms shot out and my eyes held his. He placed a brick, warm and red, in each of my palms. My unclothed body felt a tug as the weight of each brick settled into the bones of each arm.

He looked carefully at me and a slow smile spread across his face as he said, "You don't want to know what will happen if you drop these." With that, he backed away slowly, fumbling in his shirt pocket for a cigarette he was hoping to find. The corner of the room was dark as he took a seat there, and I could see the orange glow as the tip of the cigarette began to burn. Slow spirals of smoke filled the room as I stood, arms erect and holding the weight of the world in them. His outline looked like the devil had come to pay me a visit.

He had watched me—watched me for hours—and had finally succumbed to a whole liter of pulque. I had watched him drink it cup by milky cup until his mind dissolved and he lay in a stinking pile on the floor.

My mouth felt like cotton, and the blood that had caked in my eyes felt crusty and dry. The pain in my arms was something not to be told or even described. Where he had kicked me was starting to turn color and my stomach felt a vile retch as it churned its own sour juices. I hadn't shed one tear, and he had grown more and more taunting as the hours passed, frustrated that I wouldn't give him what he wanted.

I looked at him, and with a courage far beyond what I felt, I dropped the bricks and made for the door, with the harsh sounds of his drunk snoring filling the room. My arms were dead weights at my side, and I rubbed them to regain feeling. I grabbed my clothes and silently pushed the door open. It was near morning; I could see the edges of pink just beginning to color in the eastern sky.

I ran across the yard and slipped into the house. My face felt numb, and I could barely lift my arms to wash the blood away so I could see. I dressed and put some clothes into a square of fabric and tied the ends to form a pouch. I went to sit beside my mom on the bed, and gently shook her awake.

"Ma, wake up," I whispered softly. My mouth could barely open. She woke up with a start, alarm in her eyes as she saw me sitting there, my face a tangled mess.

"What are you doing? Where's your dad?" she whispered back, wincing as the blows from the night before were felt, and my heart fell slightly lower in my chest when I heard her ask for him. I realized then that she could never help me or take care of me the way she should. She was lost to me and in his grip, unable and without resources to break free of his hold. His children would be the only ones she would be allowed to care for.

I looked at her and held her hands and said, "Ma, I have to go. I can't stay here anymore because the next time he'll kill me."

She brushed her hand over my head and down over my face to my lips, fat with swelling.

"Come with me," I whispered. "Let's take the kids and get out of here. Please."

Her eyes betrayed her, and the hesitation gave me the only answer I needed. I was on my own— now and forever. I could no longer stay under his roof; my defiance to him would not be tolerated. A pang of sadness rode up my spine as I realized she was choosing him over me. I had never stood a chance.

She put some hard rolls and cheese in a small paper bag and handed it to me, while my somersaulting stomach knew that big changes were about to happen. She took her hand and in the shape of a cross blessed me from head, to heart, to chest, and back again.

"I love you, hijo," she said as she hugged me out the door.

As I slipped through the gate, the bundle of my possessions on my back, I could hear something running after me and turned to see my brother. He nearly slid into me.

"Toño, you can't leave. Not again, we just found you," he said with tears in his eyes. "Please don't leave me again." His face, my hero of a big brother, was breaking down in front of me. He was twelve and I was ten, and it had always seemed that our stations in the family were flip-flopped and I was the strong one, the older one.

"I have to go, carnal. He's going to kill me if I stay," I said, putting my hand on his shoulder to try and be brave.

We argued ferociously, with Chucho nearly dragging me back to the house. He couldn't bear life without me. When he gave up and his shoulders slumped sadly, I hugged him hard and turned away from the only faces in the world that cared about me.

My mom knew the danger I faced with my stepdad, but she could not seem to protect me. I shrugged it off, and I felt lighter and lighter as my footsteps carried me away from the madness of that house. I was ten years old and had been found less than a year earlier. And I was on my way to a new journey—one where no one would ever hurt me again.

10.

My head clear but my body hurting, I ran through several places in my mind. I remembered seeing a picture of clear waters and beautiful beaches hanging in a travel agent's office in Oaxaca. Some days I had stopped and stared at it longingly, running my finger over the soft mounds of sand with people smiling, and wishing I could go there. Maybe because I had always wanted to go back to the beach, or maybe it reminded me of my dad. I knew I wanted warmth, water, and some money jingling in my pocket.

My pockets were lined; I had taken a quick turn and dug up the money I had hidden from selling popsicles. The money I had stashed away hadn't failed me.

I got on a bus and headed toward Mexico City and the bus station that would point me south toward the Pacific Ocean. After arriving at the terminal, I meandered around, watching people and happenings. I watched people buying tickets and listened to what they said, and I soon made my way to over to purchase my own.

"Acapulco, por favor," I said smoothly, pretending to be much older than I was. The woman glanced through the window at me, never blinking, and said, "20 pesos." I fished it out of my pocket, slid it through the window, and soon was seated on a bus, waiting to go.

I fell asleep as the bus started moving and woke up several hours later to a lush landscape with palm trees and tropical foliage leaning out into the road, as if to brush the sides of the bus in welcome. I peered at the green rushing by the window. My body ached with the beating I had been dealt the night before, and I thought briefly of my mom. The sorrow I felt for her must be put away, I told myself. Only she could make the choice to leave. *I am her son*, I thought. Was I not worth leaving an abusive husband for? I knew if I let my anger run rampant that I would not succeed.

Up, up, up the bus climbed on teeming hills lined with precariously placed cement houses. The road seemed to be ready to tip us over the edge, and just when we couldn't climb any higher, we shifted downward into the bowl of the Acapulco bay. I strained my neck to see the water sparkling in the distance, and a shot of adrenaline rushed through me.

The bus stopped several blocks off the beach, and I grabbed my bag and stepped off, in search of whatever I had come searching for. Acapulco was simply a destination to a bigger plan—one that I was not completely aware of yet—but one that would soon come into my line of sight.

The air smelled of engine fuel and sand and sea, a strange and intoxicating mix that made me heady with hope. I found an entrance to the beach and ran down the stairs, and soon my feet were touching sand, instantly transported back to the days when my dad would take us to the water to play. I could feel the saltwater spread upward in my nose as I reminisced how he would throw us into the water and say, "Time to learn!" It all took me back, and yet I knew I was in the now. I was in control of my own destiny and needed to move forward.

The beach was full of tourists in the late afternoon sun, and soon enough they started heading toward their hotels to relax and head out for a cocktail and meal. I sat in the sand, watching the waves lap the shore, the sight of the beautiful bay filling my eyes.

I could see a group of kids looking slightly older than me kicking a futbol around, and I brushed off my pants and walked toward them. A ball came my direction and I kicked it back and fell into the game with a nod and a smile. We played for a while then fell back as dusk turned into evening. A fire was lit on the beach from random sticks we could find, and I soon found myself sitting beside the fire, mesmerized by its flame and the company surrounding me.

I looked at each one of these kids and took stock of them. They were slightly bedraggled, like me, and as the sun set on the bay, the fire warmed us, and they began to tell me the stories of why each one was here. There were two brothers who told of a home life so bad that living on the sand here in Acapulco was a better choice than dealing with what was left behind. The girls, tears spilling, brushed hair back from their faces as they told similar tales of unwanted and violent acts performed on them by fathers and brothers. Not sisters, they held each other like they were, and had run away and found each other, united in similar situations.

Their faces held faraway looks as they looked at me intently. My heart beat fast. Could I trust them? One of the boys said, "It's okay, man, we're familia here." I told them—from start to finish— why I had left home. I didn't consider myself a runaway because my mom knew why I had left. Still, that pang of how she could have let me go haunts me to this day. I lifted my head after the story had been told and found the group nodding with me. *We welcome you*, they smiled. *You're part of us now.*

And so I became enveloped in a group of misfits, of runaways, and of the ones whom society had forgotten. I was the youngest at ten years old, and I felt I belonged.

Bliss. I would call it bliss, in those first few days on the beaches of Acapulco. The sand was soft and it cradled my head like a soft lap. The water was warm, and my friends pulled me into their fold, like a soft sweater that feels so soothing to the touch—a balm. My untrusting heart let itself slide just a little to accommodate a new level of friendship. When you're in something together, a hard thing, the bond becomes nearly unbreakable.

The first few days I was with them, we scavenged for food and asked several vendors to give us their scraps. Bits of fish, salty and lime-flavored, slid down our throats like the sweetest of wine. I tasted my first oyster when several customers couldn't finish their plates. It burst in my mouth like so many brilliant colors that couldn't be described. Seafood and the surf in this southern port became more than I could ask for.

But as so often happens when your world is too full of good things—things that take you away from reality—my eyes were opened to what happens to survive. One night, maybe a week after I had arrived, the brothers said it was time to make some more money; it was time to go back to work for a while. I puzzled and looked at the girls, who put their heads down.

"We won't do it," one of them said. "We told you we never will."

The brothers looked at them, smiled gently. I sat with the girls and talked, afraid to ask what they had meant, when I saw the brothers emerge again. They were decked out in tight shorts and open-button shirts with their hair slicked back in the big-winged late-seventies fashion. Their legs and chests glistened with oil, and they smiled as they approached us.

"Where are you guys going to work?" I asked, innocently enough for what I had seen in my short lifetime.

"Follow us, and you'll see," one of them replied, a stark sadness in his eyes.

Resolute, they headed up the stairs to the beach. I followed behind them at a short distance. Soon, the city began to change around us, and they took short alleys and side streets to arrive at a garishly lit street filled with other similarly dressed young kids.

My heart beat loudly, and they turned around and told me to stay back, but to observe. "Maybe you'll learn how this works."

They stood by a street lamp, one on either side, and soon a parade of cars started slowly driving by. It didn't take long for me to realize that the cars held tourists who leered at me as I sat on the low wall tucked back from the street. "Hola papi, no quieres ir conmigo?" they said, as the men reached out from the cars to take a sample feel before money was handed over. I could see them running their fingers over my friends, and the blood rushed to my face, and a pair of purple high heels flashed in my brain. It brought with it everything that those girls had done to survive.

Both of the brothers tucked into cars that slid down the street and disappeared. I shrank back on my seat and hid my face from view, in disbelief, yet not surprised that they had come to this. Judgments did not come, and when they came back an hour later, they hopped out and ran over to me.

"Keep our money safe," one of them said. "We'll have a lot before the night is over. We can buy fish tomorrow!" He looked so hopeful and happy that I smiled back at him.

The other brother looked at me and said, "Several men said if you come along, you can get money, too."

I vehemently said no, but as a car pulled up and whistled, they drug me along behind them and my words faded in the night. I climbed into a car with them and two men, their blonde hair and tanned faces etched in my brain. Americans. We drove down dark streets to the white, sparkling high-rise hotels at the edge of the beach. I followed them into a side door, up an elevator, and into a hotel room. One of the men told me to sit in the corner and wait—and don't say a word.

I faded into the plush couch in the hotel room. I could hear zippers being unzipped and odd sounds coming from the bedroom area. You don't forget how certain things sound, and I remembered this sound from my early days in Oaxaca staying with the prostitutes. They had been caring and kind, but choices had limited them, and what they did for money made an imprint on me. But here I was, in a moment where time stopped, and I was brought into a space I didn't want to be in. My friends having to make choices that limited them, just to survive. One of the men came from the bedroom and looked at me, blue eyes piercing. I tried to look away, but his eyes held me.

As we all gathered to leave, my friends looked at me and motioned me to come. We climbed into the car and the engine revved; the street lights looked hazy and faraway, like a planet orbiting the sun. I felt outside of my body and wished I could be small again, reading Kaliman on a street corner in Oaxaca. But I was here, and I would be present and clear.

We rode quietly, the cobblestoned street reaching up to jostle us together, its jagged fingers finding the soft spots. Money exchanged hands, and the blonde man in the front seat tossed me a coin. I looked down at the coin and stared at its shiny face for just a bit, aware of what it would mean if I took it—then I flicked it back at him.

"No, thank you," I said. "I don't want your money."

I turned and walked back to the wall I had sat on before, and they drove away, silently slipping into the night. And as we walked home much later in the silent streets just before dawn, I vowed that I would never give my body to anyone for money, no matter how desperate I was.

The girls saw the look I held on my face and gathered me into their arms, and we fell asleep, sprawled together on the sand next to the shore.

Days and nights bled together as Acapulco embraced us, yet we knew soon it would spit us out. The streets were a cacophony of sound and happenings that twisted your soul in knots. I reasoned there was somewhere that we could go where we didn't need to hand over our souls to survive.

Several others had joined our group, and we were furtive in our daily activities so that we wouldn't get thrown off the beach where we slept. It was a place to lay a head down, but as we got larger, the danger became greater. After several months, I felt, as well, that it was time to move. The salty breeze whispered to me of new places and how to get there. Yet I wasn't sure I was ready, and so I pushed it down until I couldn't hear it anymore—until I had to listen.

"What if we headed to El Norte?" someone said, and a chill ran through my body. I had never thought of going north, and I pondered what that might mean. There was a wave of people heading north to the border; they were seeking more than the futile economy Mexico could afford them. Grown men were more and more leaving their families behind in the hopes that what lay on the other side could give them something to send home.

The legality of this never entered our minds, and my only thought was the adventure of the thing. We were a bunch of misfits with mismatched clothing and a strong will to get somewhere. The idea settled in my gut and rolled around. I had nothing here, nor anywhere, and I was free to decide what I wanted and where I wanted to go.

"Let's do it," I said breathlessly, a stirring deep inside me. They all looked at me, with the fire we circled lighting up their faces. "I think we should go," I said again, catching my breath and knowing that it was right. It was what needed to happen.

"Okay," said one of the brothers. "We go north."

And as the morning chill burned off with the sun's rising, our backs were already turned and we were walking swiftly, heading up, up, upward toward a destination that called us.

El Norte.

11.

Across the river. What would I find there? *El Norte.* I rolled those two words around in my mouth as a strange wave of calmness found rest in my heart. Was this a place I could finally call home? I could help my mom—maybe, just a little. Most of all, I wanted success and a place to lay my head.

Excitement filled me as my feet trod the rocky surface of the road. I turned my body around and glimpsed the Acapulco bay disappear over the hill, and stuck out my thumb and waited for a ride as my feet moved, one step at a time. Hitch-hiking was common in Mexico during that time period, and if anything, Mexicans are friendly. Anytime a truck with an open bed passed by, we could be sure they would stop to take us along wherever they were headed. The back of a truck could be made comfortable by nestling your blanket in the corner and wrapping the front around you, with your bundle of clothes to lay your head on. A shock absorber, I called it, as the trucks made their way over the notoriously bumpy terrain.

The verdant mountains in the southern state Guerrero were immense to my mind, and I took in every square inch as we passed through. At night when it became too dark to travel, I would stretch my blanket between two trees and create a hammock to lie in under the stars. I would let my mind travel through the sky and find each constellation. It kept me grounded, the night sky, in an ever-changing landscape of spaces and people. It was a constant reminder that somewhere up there in the vastness that was my life, God was still looking over me. He was there whether I was lost or on the road to an uncertain destination. My life seemed destined to always be moving, never to have one place to call home.

My fellow band of travelers was the closest thing I had to home. As we traveled from Guerrero through the state of Mexico, into a small part of Hidalgo, and through Querétaro and San Luis Potosi, we became a tight-knit group that looked out for each other.

At night, when camping in whatever empty space we could find, we told stories to cling to bits of the past. I recalled my mom and dad when I was little and my big brother Chucho. They were the only things important to me, and when that long-ago life was shattered, it was as if my soul could never be patched together again. An ache spread through me, and I curled up in my blanket and let the night cover me.

The landscape changed as we slowly made our way into the north via strangers who became friends. Dusty plains with scrub brush flashed by, and as we moved north into Nuevo León and around the city of Monterrey, I sensed a bit of dread moving through me. We all looked at each other as unfamiliar territory seemed to be overtaking us, and for the first time, doubts began to rise.

"Why are we really crossing the border?" one of the girls said, her frame small and insular as she crossed her arms. It was the first time that we had uttered the name—frontera, border. It was the end of the road, or was it the beginning?

I looked at her and said, "I can't say why I want to go. A fresh start? A better place to call home where no one can hurt us?" The wheels spun in my mind, thinking of all the ideas I had, because it never stopped thinking. My brain worked like a computer constantly spitting out data, always something new.

She looked down and her lip quivered as tears formed in her eyes. I put my arm around her and left it there. My attempt at compassion was met with eyes that smiled at me, but a smile that never quite reached her mouth.

Tamaulipas met us with more desert and scrub brush and hearts pounding hard inside us. We had split up our group and were riding in the back of two separate trucks, pushing forward with no promise of going back. We were dropped off at a church, its terracotta expanse cool to the touch in the last light of day.

I could see the stars starting to peep out of the sky and was comforted as thoughts of what lay ahead taunted me. Why was I leaving Mexico, the only place I had ever known? I captured my thoughts and knew, without one doubt, that this was right. Move forward. Don't look back. Our group wasn't going to search out a dream. We were going for the adventure, and in the back of our minds, to possibly find a softer place to call home.

We awaited the arrival of the other truck and settled in to wait for darkest night and the completion of a long trip. Our faces were haggard and worn, yet hopeful. The United States. What did I think it would be? I huddled under my blanket and fell fast asleep.

The climate in the United States today is one of vicious disdain aimed at border security, invasion, and over-population. Anger, when seen coming from someone who doesn't have all the facts, causes me to pause.

If I could explain why so many Mexicans—me included—want to cross to the United States, one would only have to look at some of the conditions that my people live in. It's a choice they make to change their lives, sometimes a desperate choice. When was the last time you had to decide the future of your family, to keep them safe at all costs, whether they live better or spiral into the hands of crippling poverty? Into inescapable oppression by those in power? Life hands us hard decisions to make, and like a boat adrift at sea, we often need a port.

In the late seventies, I was one of many who took my future into my own hands, rolled it around a bit, then made the decision to swim that river. Sadly, many have told me to swim back across to Mexico and stay there. I want you to think back over forty years and consider what you were doing then. Did ten-year-old Toño being here affect your life in any way? If you can't say that it did then and can't say that it does now, then it's time to put your anger away. If you think it did, then put this book down and stop reading.

I was jolted awake by a rough shake of my shoulders.

"Wake up! Time to go!" said my friend Gordo, one of several who had joined us somewhere along the trail north. I sat bolt upright and grabbed my bag, tucking all its contents inside a plastic bag I had found in the trash along the road.

My eyes took in the commotion around me as we readied ourselves for this perilous trek, one that would change our lives. Nothing prepares you for something you've never done. You go by words and advice people might give you, but the act itself? It must be done and done alone.

Our group of ten or so slipped quietly down the darkened streets toward the river. As we approached, we could see what can only be described as a graveyard of belongings. The shore was littered with personal effects like clothing, a random shoe, or a doll that was left behind.

My veins throbbed with increased blood pressure, and I looked beyond the river. I could see twinkling lights, and they were pulsing and calling my name. *Toño, come see us. We're waiting for you.* The lights looked brighter than any I had seen in Mexico. They were garish to my eyes and grew wavy and distant as I tried to focus on their intensity.

Would the United States be kind to me? Would I ever see my mom again? I tucked those thoughts into the plastic bag that was now open and being stuffed with the clothes I had on my back. My underwear was dingy gray, having been worn for so long, and I covered my chest with my arms.

Our group stood on the shore clad only in our underthings and gripping plastic bags tightly, like it was the last thing we had to hold onto.

"Make sure you swim straight and fast," Gordo said. "There are small whirlpools in the river that will suck you straight down." I glanced out and saw the river moving swiftly. The water was dark. I wasn't afraid, though. I was exhilarated.

My toes dipped in the water. It was January and the water was freezing, but we surged in, nothing behind or ahead to stop us. The bank on the other side was empty, and night sounds of calling birds bounced off the water's surface. Life on this side of an imaginary line was fading from view. My body slowly slipped into the Rio Grande, and my head soon began bobbing at the surface. If I didn't recognize this as a serious moment, a life-altering thing, then forgive me. I was nearing eleven years old and had lived a lifetime of serious moments disguised as my life.

With Gordo in front of me, I clenched my bag

tightly and began to swim, one-armed, against the current. Behind me, I could hear splashes and grunts as the brothers and girls, along with the others who had joined us, entered the shivery water. Time stood still as the water pressed against me. Gasps and short screams burst out, along with long shushes to quiet us. "Immigration is all around!" some whispered sharply.

I could feel my lungs start to ache along with my body as I swam as fast as my legs and arms could take me. My dad had taught me to swim well. I could see the shore, as we were nearing halfway across, and I longed to step my foot on it. I didn't think, I just kept going, and I knew I would make it.

Suddenly, giant swells of screams welled up behind us along with shouts for help. I glanced around and with horror saw a dark head going under, bobbing like a cork in a swirling tub. Faces looked forward to me, with frantic arms waving to come back.

Gordo whispered heavily back to me, "We

can't go back. We can't help them. If we try, we will drown as well."

A tingle went up my cold spine as the screams turned to wailing. Then I heard a shot, a bullet that came from somewhere beyond my sight. I heard it hit as more screams and gurgles issued from my friends. I shut my ears and struggled against the pull of the river, the hard undercurrent pulling like frozen fingers under the surface.

I believe many times in my life I should have died. I sometimes think I should have died that first night crossing over. But I clung to the fact that God knew my name, a small boy who lived in the in-between spaces of this life.

As my feet stumbled on hard footing, I drug myself up onto the scrubby riverbank, and for the first time I set foot on U.S. soil. Gordo was in the bushes, telling me to get hidden, to hurry up. I looked back across the expanse of river and could see several of my friends on the other side who were crying and holding each other. Someone had lost their life, we didn't know who, and the others were unaccounted for. A distance of twenty feet had separated us.

I turned back to Gordo, who was putting on his clothes and already heading up the side of the bank. He looked back at me urgently, spurring me on. I donned my clothes and followed him, securing my bag of belongings tightly to my wrist. I never saw my other friends again.

My heart was pounding as I slipped up the side of the bank, screams subsiding in the distance as we crept further from the river. Distance, we need distance, he kept saying as the brush scratched my arms and legs, the mindless stinging not noticed. I banished from my mind the thought of one of my friends dying, lost in the swirling rush of the water. I shook my head as if to clear it and pressed on, until we came to a slight clearing where I could see train tracks standing stark in the moonlight.

"Help me dig a hole big enough to lay in," said Gordo, and we scavenged for anything to dig with. We used sticks, our hands, and random pieces of metal that had been discarded. After what seemed an enormous amount of time, we had a shallow hole big enough for both of us.

"I want you to lay here and keep your head down," he said. "And when I say 'jump out and run,' you jump out and run as fast as you can for the train." Trains were a thread that ran through my life, carrying me to distant places and things, and tonight was just one in a succession. I never stopped to consider whether I could die or why I was doing this thing I was doing, but I screwed up my courage and looked ahead to what the next minutes would bring.

"The train will pass, then stop and go in reverse. They do this to catch people who are jumping the trains," Gordo said. "But when it moves forward for the third time, it will take off faster. Be ready." I knew he had crossed the border several times and was giving me good advice. I was thankful, but couldn't help remembering my brother telling me, "You better follow or you'll be left behind."

I shivered and lay down in the shallow hole with Gordo beside me, as he pulled long slats of wood for camouflage over the top of us. My breathing shallowed, and I willed myself to stay still. And we waited.

A whistle pierced my skull and I woke up with a start. Gordo was peering through the slats in the wood, and he looked at me and told me to get up and watch. I looked with one eye and could see the train stopping and backing up as bodies scattered in every direction. Men with guns ran them down and caught them as the train moved forward again and back once more. I could see them being led into a waiting truck where numerous heads were bowed in defeat. *I won't be one of them*, I promised myself.

We were a good one hundred feet up from where the train had stopped, and as it shuddered to move forward for the third time, Gordo looked at me and nodded his head. *Be ready.* He mouthed the words, and I grabbed my bag and held onto it like it was the last thing I would own.

The train gathered steam as the conductor's face flashed past us, ready to move north. Seconds felt like hours, and suddenly Gordo threw off the slats and took off at a gallop. He never looked back at me, only at his destination right in front of him.

I jumped out and started running, adrenaline taking over as I neared the hot beast of iron. I looked up and saw Gordo swing himself into a car and look back for me. Was it instinct, or was there a hand on me every step I took? The wheels turned dizzyingly in front of my eyes, and I knew I needed to make the leap to catch on. The train was picking up speed, and soon I would run out of space to run. The metal turned hazy, like a speeding bullet, and I jumped forward with every muscle straining to grab on—

I caught a handle and could instantly feel the forces dragging my body back, back, as a kite blows in the wind. I pulled hard, and my foot found purchase. I hung on for dear life. In all my life, I've never felt an exhilaration like I felt when I jumped on that train on a dark night in south Texas.

I swung myself up, the wind whooshing by me, and landed on my feet inside the train car. Gordo looked at me and shook his head and said, "I've never seen anyone make that jump the first time." My lungs filled with oxygen and I looked out at the spinning night, dark with scrub that looked like the Mexico we had just left behind. I could feel my entire life flying beside me, whipping in the wind. The tracks were leading us north to San Antonio, Texas, and hurtling me toward my destiny.

12.

Like a tumbleweed blowing across a vast plain, I felt my life moving forward at lightning speed. I felt I had lived a lifetime in my nearly eleven short years, years that should have been full of security. I never look back on my life and wish things had been different. Each separate thing made me into the person I was. Did it make me a better person? The years that lay ahead of me would try every ounce of positive energy I had.

The landscape of my life was changing, moving me toward a place and country where I had never been. In the dark cocoon of the train, I slumbered with messy dreams of dark waters, friends I had lost, and blows to the head.

When I awoke, we were gliding into a city that lay nestled in gentle green hills. Gordo was by the door, and he told me to get ready to jump. "Don't even think about it, and don't try to land on your feet. Let your body embrace the ground and roll," he said, as he held his bag tighter.

As we rounded a slight corner and could see buildings flashing by, he looked at me and said, "Go!" He jumped off, and I could see him tumbling over and over.

I gauged the distance and I jumped, letting the ground hit my shoulders first to absorb the shock. I rolled and popped up, looking at my arms and legs to make sure I was in one piece. The sun was peeking over the horizon, and her brilliant colors lit the sky with their warmth. I gazed in wonder at the sight. *Couldn't this be for me*, I thought? The thoughts slid out and into the atmosphere to float upward where maybe, just maybe, someone might capture them and hear the plea.

I walked in a strange land with buildings that had wooden sides and peaked roofs. I gazed in wonder at the absence of fences around houses and at streets that didn't end in dusty, pothole-filled roads. Instead, I saw asphalt streets that glittered in the morning sun, as well as concrete sidewalks that were just beginning to fill with people heading to work or school. Jean-clad children with book bags and freshly combed hair chattered as they walked the tree-lined sidewalks that led to school. I breathed in the air that for the first time, fully, I realized wasn't air that swirled over the land of my birth. I was in the United States, and I could hear what could only be English being spoken as we walked silently by, trying not to draw notice.

My face was covered with a layer of soot, and, not for the first time, hunger gnawed at my stomach. I never asked Gordo if he'd been here before; I never thought to ask him anything because when I turned to see if we might find something to eat, he was gone. There are times I wonder if he was really with me, crossed with me, encouraged me on when I wanted to turn back, taught me how to jump the train, and helped me arrive safely at the destination. I stood and looked around, and he had simply vanished, leaving me standing alone on the street corner.

I clutched my bag and started walking, hoping to find a friendly face.

The streets looked all the same and began to blend together. Palm trees dotted the landscape and soon the pains were overtaking my belly. I saw a sign that said "Tacos" and thought I would try my luck, dirty face or not.

The place was tiny, with several tables and chairs and a long bar with high stools to sit on. I climbed up on a stool and looked at the waitress expectantly.

"Honey, you on your way to school?" she said, as her blue eyeshadow crinkled in the corners of her eyes. Dark eyeliner and even darker hair complemented the orange of her uniform, and I simply nodded my head. She cocked her head carefully, and asked me in Spanish, "Tienes hambre? Are you hungry?"

The look of relief on my face must have registered with her, and soon she was setting down a big glass of milk and a plate with eggs and toast. I wolfed it down, not even stopping to breathe.

"Despacio! Slowly!" she said and smiled even bigger. She was the first American I had talked to. I could do this. After she showed me the restroom and I washed my face, she hustled me out the door. She handed me several rolls tucked in a napkin and put a hand to her lips in the universal *Shhh* sign.

My stomach full, I looked at my surroundings. I knew I had to be careful; I was still young enough to be caught. I was growing, though, my legs were longer and I felt older—older because of life experience? I don't know. I felt exhilaration at my conquest, my search for more and better. I wanted to travel the world, to make money, and to be the best me I could be.

As I walked down a street, I noticed several boys around my age, some older, gazing out at me from a small caravan of empty semi-truck trailers. A fruit market was set up in front, and I wandered around it and eyeballed the kids, wondering who they belonged to. Were things done differently around here? I never gave it a thought that they might be on their own, but when I struck up a conversation with them, I found that they were. Soon, a little crowd surrounded me, and I realized that all of them spoke Spanish.

"What's your name? Where are you from?" they asked me, curious.

My favorite movie star in Mexico had always been Jorge Rivero. He starred in many western movies, and he was my idol. I had watched his movies over and over, and with his cool, calm ways, he was an example to me. I rolled it around on my tongue and found myself saying, "Jorge. My name is Jorge." A new name for a new place— it made sense and I went with it. "My family is from Teotihuacán, but I traveled from Acapulco to come here," I said. "Who are you guys?"

Stories poured out of them, as their faces told the tale of harrowing rides and near-death experiences. I could see the homesickness inside of them, and I'll admit I felt it, too. I put my chin up, though, and the leader-of-the-pack instinct came out once again. A strange sense of a changing of ways, of making things different, overcame me. I could sense fear in some of them for the way they had been living, so they were drawn to me, to my confidence.

"Can I stay here with you guys?" I asked. I heard yes many times over, and soon I was shown a corner of a trailer where I laid down my bag.

I spent the day helping the fruit vendors in this very small market. They allowed us to help with menial tasks for a small price. This small price allowed us to buy some bananas from them and to use the hose to wash off. I was dead tired and falling over from exhaustion as I laid my head on my bag. I had a roof over my head, albeit a tin one, but it was still a roof. My expectations for San

Antonio were not yet known, but I knew wherever I was, I would find the best part of it.

These first few years in the United States were fluid, and they passed by. My life consisted of staying in the trailer with friends, many nights spent talking about the homes we left behind. We had left for different choices, different reasons. Many had left to seek a new way of life, to leave behind homes filled with harsh living and extreme poverty. For others, parents had encouraged them to leave as a means of helping the family. They expected them to work and send the money back home. Me? I left on a whim, a challenge, a way to better myself and see new things in the process. When life leaves you battered, you want nothing more than to come up for air someplace new. I knew when I became successful that I would help my mom, but for now, I had done it for me.

In those first few years, I found that living in San Antonio wasn't hard. I lived on the west side of the city, which was predominantly Latino, or in another word, Chicano—which is how I came to know them. Chicanos are Mexican-Americans, and while American-born, they identify fully with their cultural heritage. Native English speakers, they also talk a mixture of what I came to know as Spanglish. Spanglish combines both the Spanish and English language, seamlessly blending both as it rolls off the tongue. I heard Spanish spoken every day, though, and as a result, I didn't have to learn English immediately. When I woke up, I could hear lilting voices coming from open windows, as well as people walking down the street. Various English words and phrases came to me, as in "How are you?" "What is your name?" "My name is Jorge," and so forth. I was a quick study, and I soon was comfortable going into small stores to purchase things I needed.

My everyday life consisted of a routine that went something like this: Get up, wash my face and as much of my body as I could with a hose that was nearby, start a small fire in a pit we had, cook eggs over the fire, along with a piece of bread. I have always been a tidy person and like to keep where I stay clean and neat. Appearance is everything to getting ahead in life and is the first thing people see of you. I kept that principle and held it close. After folding my blanket and covering up my belongings with it, I began my day.

Our group came in at around ten boys ranging in age from eleven to sixteen, and the fruit vendors were always grateful for our help. They never asked us where we came from; they just extended a smile and gave us crates to stack, rotten fruit to dispose of, or a job carrying new shipments off large trucks that came to deliver. I made myself useful and in doing so became indispensable. When you are quick to smile and have ready hands, your road will take you farther.

The United States became a familiar place, and I knew that I would make my home here. I wanted to move to different states and see the scenery and get to know the people, because the opportunities seemed endless. School, for as little as I had gone, was a blip on the radar of my past. I knew I didn't need it to succeed because I knew who I was and what my abilities were. I was cocky, yes, as well as confident.

As years passed, though, I found myself wanting to see my mom and my brother again. Life is fleeting, I knew, and somewhere along the way to age thirteen, I decided I would go home and visit.

When you're on your own and living on the streets, you don't always see how you look, how you're growing. Quick flashes of myself in the mirror in restrooms or in the way girls were beginning to look me over gave me a clue to the changes. I never learned about puberty until my own body started to make changes like hair under my arms and a deepening of my voice. As I worked at whatever came my way each day, my muscles had begun to form and grow, and when I had the opportunity to see a reflection the changes were evident. I was growing into a man.

After two years living in San Antonio and nothing more exciting happening than a day at the zoo, I hopped on a bus using money saved from working odd jobs and headed south. Fleeting thoughts of my stepdad went through my head like a slideshow, but I didn't care. He couldn't hurt me now because I was as big as him. If anything, he should be scared of me.

If you're wondering what happens when you are undocumented and return to the country of your birth, the answer is, well, nothing. They wave you through and you keep on going. It's the return trip that would bring me once again to that rushing river, but I banished that thought from my mind as I grew more excited at seeing my mom. It seems that no matter the transgression, you can forgive the people you love. Her staying with my stepdad and not saving me instead had felt unforgiveable. I took that thought and caught it up in my hand, then opened my fingers and blew. Holding onto past pains only served to make you weak. I was strong, invincible even, and needed to stay that way to survive.

The buses in Mexico are an adventure, because if you know anything about driving there, you know to simply close your eyes and hold on. The roads were narrow, with no berms, but that never stopped a car from passing between your bus and the bus coming the opposite direction. It was always and still is a death race when entering traffic, and you just sit back and enjoy the ride.

As the northern states of Mexico flashed by, I fell asleep, lulled by the thought of being with my family that night. Was I hoping things had changed?

13.

The bus pulled into the teeming square of San Juan, Teotihuacán, and I looked around to take it in. Smallish in size, it was a bustling town that prided itself on the ancient pyramids that sat not one mile outside the city limits. They were built by a people that are unknown, yet it was a major center in the ancient world, becoming established around 100 BC. The city became a ghost town some 1500 years ago, and the Aztec people renamed it *Teotihuacán* which means, "The place where the gods meet." I remembered running those pyramids several years back and how we had made money selling popsicles. The memory stung me.

My chest felt tight, and I checked myself in the glass at the front of a store. My hair was wavy and combed back in the style of 1980, and I had on a pair of blue jeans and a light blue shirt. I looked completely different than when I had left. I had matured quickly; some boys don't until they're much older, but not me. Maybe nature had a way of helping me along so I could deal with life on my own at a very young age. I had grown into myself and I liked it.

I caught a taxi and headed to the white house. My palms were slightly sweaty, and I wondered what had changed. *Will they have cared where I've been all these years?* As we pulled onto the lane, the one I had walked away from nearly three years ago, we stopped in front of the gate. I paid the driver and got out, then slowly walked around and inside toward the house.

I saw two children playing outside, banging around with sticks and rocks. A white husky dog yipped playfully and barked when he saw me. I patted him on the head and looked deep into his eyes. The kids looked up at me. I looked back at them, and they walked toward me with curiosity, and I began speaking to them. I said, "I'm your brother." They smiled, those toothy grins that little kids have, and I saw a woman walk out of the house. She was heavily pregnant with a third baby, which would make a total of seven pregnancies for her. She looked tired, but when she turned to look at me, her eyes lit up and she burst into tears. It was my mom.

"Mijo! Oh my God, Toño!" She came to me, and we embraced, a long hug of reconciliation and sorrow. She touched my face, and the tears streamed down hers.

"Ma, it's okay. Don't cry," I said. "I just needed to see you again. And Chucho. Where is he?" He wasn't home from school, she said, and my stepdad was due home any time.

We went into the house, and it was bare as an empty cupboard. They had managed to buy a bed, but there were still sleeping mats on the floor. The stove was falling apart, and the table was a board across cement blocks. But I could smell a pot of beans cooking on the stove and warm tortillas sat inside a damp cloth.

"Sit down," she said, moving with a cumbersome gait. "I'll fix you something to eat." There would be plenty of time to talk of where I had been, what I was doing. A plate filled with beans, hot and fragrant, was set in front of me and several tortillas were put on the burner to char. As I scooped my first bite, I could taste home and what I had missed by leaving. Yet leaving had been the only way to be out from my stepdad's control.

Just that quick, my brother Chucho came in the door and looked at me with a shocked expression, then dropped everything and ran to me. We hugged and no words were said; we just hugged. The white dog barked loudly and Chucho turned to him and said, "Hey Oso, I see you've met Toño!" Oso, which means *bear*, would become my closest ally. Every time I returned home, he'd be waiting to greet me.

They both exclaimed how old I looked, and my mom said I was so handsome, that I looked like my dad. Her tears came, and she covered her face with her hands. I let her cry because I knew when she lost my dad and both children that her life had turned upside down. If only she could see that my stepdad was not the person she needed in her life.

"Ma, how is Dad treating you? Is he hitting you all the time?" Her hands still covered her eyes, but she slowly brought them down and wiped her tears with a sleeve. She looked at me and shook her head. Chucho put his head down, as if defeat had taken over him. He was in his last year of high school and just wanted to finish it and get on with his life. He looked at Mom, and I knew then and there that it had gotten worse, that my stepdad had turned even more on my mom. "Ma, you can leave. Let me take you back to live with Tio Alvaro," I implored. "Let me help you."

She shook her head vehemently and shifted

her bulk in the seat. The two little ones clung to her and she put her hand on their heads, almost as if to say that she could never leave. I believe she was thinking of the ones she had lost, as well as me. There was too much at stake, and yet I shook my head. Was I the price she had to pay?

Lourdes and Armando, the two littlest, looked at me with their big eyes, and I held out my arms to them. One by one they came and sat with me, their dark hair spilling onto my chest. I knew she would never leave.

We talked late into the evening, the candle on the table burning down, down until there was nothing left but the wick. I looked at Chucho, and he motioned me outside.

"Pa isn't home. We need to go find him," he said. "Come with me."

I knew what he meant. My stepdad was drunk again and passed out somewhere on the street. A child with an alcoholic father has a burden to carry. A wife with an abusive, alcoholic husband carries twice the burden. I clenched my fists and followed him out the door. *Let him rot on the street corner*, my thoughts told me.

We traveled on the lane, looking in every corner and patch of cement. About one half mile down the road, we came upon a group of men drinking pulque, their weapon of choice. They were in a tight group, smoke curling up around them and disappearing into the darkened sky. Eyes glazed, they tried to concentrate on our faces, but the effort was causing them too much trouble.

"Have you seen my dad?" Chucho asked. They did a head nod to the side, and there was my stepdad, lying half on the sidewalk and half in the weeds. He was passed out and snoring heavily with a container empty of drink clutched tightly to his chest.

Chucho went over to him and started shaking him roughly to wake up. "Pa, Pa! Wake up. Let's go home."

My brother looked at me and implored me to help him. I knew he had been dealing with this alone; he had been the one to always stay home and take care of things. My mom, as upset as she got with her husband, never dared to find him. A woman showing up to drag home her husband when he's drinking, at least in those years, was not something that was done.

As angry as I still was at my dad, I loved my brother. *Pissed*, that was the word that described my emotions when I thought about all this man had made my mom and my brother go through. I walked over and grabbed his other arm and said, "Orale, Jefe. Let's go!"

He looked at me, eyes not comprehending what they saw, and he tried to shake us off. He squinted, and we lifted him and each put one arm around him as we carted him off. He smelled like death warmed over, as urine and days of drinking blended together to create a dirty potpourri. I turned my head and kept telling myself that I was doing it for my mom, for Chucho, and for my little brother and my sister. But what good was it if nothing changed? If he could never be the husband or father that anyone needed?

After we had deposited him at home with my mom, my brother and I sat outside and talked. Chucho had dreams, and I knew he might never reach them. Just like my mom, he couldn't leave home—it wasn't built into him. We talked of school and of his good grades, of girls and the many dates he went on. He was a handsome guy, and the girls loved him. He would slick back his hair when he went to dances, and I thought he looked like Elvis come back to life. I hated the life he had to live with my dad.

"Does he hit you?" I asked, hoping the answer would be truthful.

"Not really. He just doesn't think I know how to do anything," he said, hanging his head. I knew this to be true; my stepdad always had a way of making people feel inferior, as if the knowledge they had was miniscule compared to his.

Chucho was the kind of person who would take it from him, then go out and relieve his tension by doing other things. He was quick, my brother, and I found out he had made a reputation for being a great fighter. These streets meant that you let people know who you were, and fighting went along with it. He had regaled me with stories of dances and the scuffles that occurred afterwards. I looked at him and said, "I'm sorry I had to go. We both know he would have killed me. Pinche cabrón." I pinched my nose and shook off the feeling.

Chucho shook his head and opened his mouth to speak, then shut it again. He looked up at the sky and then straight at me. "I love you, Toño. You know that. All we've gone through together. I'm so sorry you had to leave."

Tears sprang to my eyes, and we grabbed each other's hand roughly. How had we both grown up? Him nearing adulthood and living in a volatile home, and myself living in the United States. It was something we wouldn't have guessed and wouldn't have wanted to guess. My brother was everything to me, and when I looked at him, I could still see us playing on the beach with Dad. My life wasn't destined for easy. I knew that.

We went back in and lay down on the mats, and soon he was sleeping soundly. I looked up at the ceiling and met the night for many hours before I could sleep.

I heard him before I saw him, mumbling loudly, "Eva, where is my café? I want frijoles and eggs." My mom scurried, quickly setting out the breakfast things as his coherence returned, slowly and with an ever-expanding awareness of his surroundings. I got up and folded up the blanket and walked into the kitchen where he sat at the table. His eyes, yellow and still alcohol-glazed, looked me over.

"Well, look who is here." I was bigger, much bigger, though still only thirteen. He took in my broadened shoulders and muscular arms and looked back at my eyes. "What brings you back here to our poor house?"

There were those words, *pobre casa,* that so

many use to describe their dwelling or really, their way of life. It is a way of being self-deprecatory, but in a jesting way. I hated it. It did nothing but bring pity to who you were, and no matter what your house or clothing looked like, you have to stand proud—it's the only way to be confident in your life.

"Hello to you, too, Pa," I said, the word *Pa* grating my tongue as it came out.

"So, tell me where you've been since you left us so long ago?" he said, and his tone indicated he would believe only what he wanted.

"I went to Acapulco for a time, then I hitchhiked north with friends and crossed the river. I've been living in San Antonio," I said. I was proud of where I had taken myself. I was better off than I had ever been with him.

He threw back his head and laughed until my face grew hard. I wouldn't let him get to me, I just wouldn't.

"Don't you mean San Antonio de las Palmas?" he said. "That's just a short way from here. I don't

believe you ever made it to los Estados Unidos."
He looked at me, piercing me with the bait I
refused to take. Every second I had ever spent
with him had been a series of jabs and punches—
and him being right on all counts.

I looked at him calmly, trying to outstep him,
and replied, "No, I meant San Antonio, Texas. I've
been there for several years now."

His eyes narrowed as a slow smile stretched
across his face. "You know, lying to us doesn't
make it true." I could sense my mom growing
tense as she poured the coffee and set three cups
and a bowl of sugar on the table.

"Sit down and eat," she said. "All three of
you." Looking at Chucho, she motioned him to sit
down. I picked up a spoon and stirred several
spoonsful of sugar into the cup, carefully
watching it swirl until it came to a dead stop.

I looked up at him and said, "You can think
I'm lying if you want to, but I've been living in
San Antonio, Texas. Just because you say I'm lying
doesn't mean I am."

Our eyes held each other, and in that moment, just for a fraction of a second, I could see that I had won. He had registered and filed away how much bigger I was and the way that I answered him. A flicker of fear flashed in his eyes, barely noticeable, but I saw it.

He turned his head away from me and picked up his coffee and began to drink. When the charred tortillas were delivered to the table, he tucked his head and began to eat. He didn't say another word.

I stayed a couple of weeks, and then I knew it was time to go. My stepdad had left me alone, but I could see that my being there caused him to be uncomfortable. My mom grew braver when I was there, now that I had grown bigger and older, and she didn't want me to go.

"Please stay," she said, sorrow in her eyes along with a stroke of panic.

"Ma, it's time for me to go," I said, the words sounding of freedom from this place. "I'm headed to Acapulco for a little while. I might stop on the way back." She shook her head, and tears welled up, and I added, "You don't have to stay here. He's terrible to you."

In the time I was there, I could hear them talking in the mornings, or outside, when they thought I couldn't hear. Theirs was the best example I could give of the abuser/victim relationship. Manipulation was key in getting her to remain with him, and she feared him just as much as she loved him. It was a circle that went round and round until someone grew too dizzy and flew off and got hurt. If she didn't have his pants washed and hung out to dry, a fist would come. No beans cooked and ready to eat? Another smack. His words, terrible and slow, would rake her over and over until I could see the defeat in her eyes and the sorrowful, to me, obeisance that she gave him. It was undeserved. He was king of nothing, not to any of the children he sired, nothing. He would never get my respect.

I waited for her to respond, and when she didn't, she walked up to me and with her hand touched me with the stations of the cross. A kiss on the forehead was brushed lightly, and as she lowered her hands to rest on her swollen belly, I turned to leave. The little kids clung to me as I left the gate, Chucho at my side, and we turned to walk to the bus station.

"When will you come back?" he asked, as we entered the town square where the buses were lined up.

"I may stop on the way back through; and if not, I'll try to make my way home every year."

We hugged, harsh and brief, and I climbed in with my knapsack on my back. He waved, and I watched his face grow smaller and smaller. I was always saying goodbye.

14.

Even with goodbyes, lost friends, and loneliness in my lifetime, I loved every day. Excitement surged through me as the bus headed south to Acapulco. I was older, wiser, and ready to see what I could find. Although I knew I would return to the United States, I felt the itch to travel. The bus chugged though the same tropical landscape that had taken me to Acapulco several years before, and when we crested the mountain, I smiled. The city had been eye-opening, and this time I was ready for it.

I didn't have a plan, and I hopped out of the bus and went down the steps to the beach. The waves ravished the shore as the sun started its descent, and I took a deep breath and laid my head on the sand. I never failed to thank God for all the good things he brought me, despite everything.

My mom's face came to mind, and I thought about all the choices she had had to make—pregnant and alone, marrying my dad, picking up and taking a risk for Chucho and myself, and now choosing to stay with my stepdad when the future looked bleak. We all have choices, and none of us are to blame for the other, but my mom was now thirty-six years old and still growing the family. Were these her dreams, or had she just rolled with the tide of life, never really having a choice? *I will always have a choice*, my thoughts said, *I will never be put where I don't want to be, never*.

I slept in the sand that night, alone with my thoughts. When the day broke, I sat up and glanced at the bay. Beams of light were just beginning to stretch over the water, and I got up to begin my day.

I walked with purpose down the hot, sticky streets, and it wasn't long before I met up with a group of kids—kids like me—who were banded together by situation. We talked, and soon I had a place to stay for a few days.

I wanted to work, so I went into some of the bars and restaurants that lined the beach and soon had a job helping a bartender. In Mexico, there is no drinking age, and I had a face that said "hard worker," so I was hired on the spot. Later that evening, I arrived with my best clothes on and they put me to work.

The club was called Disco Beach, and it sat right near the water's edge. It was 1980, and the disco music was pumping out onto the sand, the bass booming, as people started arriving. The bartender put me to work slicing limes, and it was there in the dimly lit bar of Disco Beach that I learned how to properly cut the juicy green orbs so the slice would fit into the drinks. I cut oranges and mint, filled the ice buckets, and ran for more glasses when we ran out. The club was like a heartbeat trapped inside a small area, and I watched the crowd, mesmerized by their dancing and wildly gyrating bodies.

Several nights in, I mixed my first drink and soon was king of the blender. I would mix and bring it to the bartender to pour. He had flair. He would pour the blended liquid into a silver shaker and do a little dance as he melded the ingredients into tropical goodness. Some evenings I was given the privilege of taking the drinks out to customers, and if there was a tip given, he would let me have it.

I worked hard and learned by watching to play even harder. The Acapulco night scene was lively, and I was privy to lots of conversations because of one thing—I paid attention. I overheard groups of girls planning to meet a group of guys later at the hotel, trysts were whispered in ears and decided upon, and drugs in tiny packages were exchanged at the bar counter and in the tight spaces of stairways, bathrooms, and corners. It was all there to see, and when people are on vacation, they seem to lose their inhibitions. Several times I walked in on club-goers having sex in the restroom or on the sand one step off the club's dance floor. I had men ask me to pose for pictures, wanting me to put on smallish trunks, their eyes leering. Did I know why they wanted the pictures? Not at the time, but I saw many girls in these types of situations, paraded in as we waited our turn to pose; and I knew one might never see their faces again if they weren't smart. It was a heady mix for a thirteen-year-old boy, not quite a man. But it was also money to be made for simply standing there. I learned what I should do and what I shouldn't do, although in years to come the line would be blurred by bad choices and unsound reasoning. But for now, I was cajoled sweetly into this life, moment by moment, and it made me feel alive.

After work wound down in the small hours of the night, I was given a small cut. Counting my money, I walked to whatever friend's house I was staying with for the night—or whatever was left of the night. The lights on the hills surrounding the Acapulco Bay twinkled like glitter strewn with a heavy hand. The sea filled my nostrils as the crusty streets turned into even tinier ones until I would find the floor or couch that was mine to curl up on.

It was a nomadic existence, and I was thriving. I would sleep no longer than nine because I've always felt that if I don't get up, I'll miss the day. I still feel that way today. My friends were usually still sleeping, heaped one, two, and three beside each other as I slipped into the restroom. A shower or sponge bath, and I was out the door to find breakfast.

I took myself down to the plaza where many vendors were set up, and I would sit down and order a very large glass of freshly squeezed orange juice. This isn't just any orange juice; it's each orange, peeled with knowing hands, placed in a hand squeezer, and squished—plump sections bursting while the juice runs down into a basin. It's then poured into a tall, clear glass and served. The juice would wash down my throat like the sweetest nectar, and I would move on to the next stall and order a bolillo with egg and cheese. I made sure that my stomach was full.

Working gave me a sense of satisfaction, yet I knew there was more to be had in different ways, a set of actions that I hadn't yet taken or thought of. My mind was churning endlessly, so to stop the motion, I would go to the beach and play soccer with my friends. We'd discard our shirts and the sun would scorch our backs as our muscles grew strong, running and jumping in the sand with the ball. We were young, wild, and full of life. Girls—locals and tourists—would stop and watch us play. I knew they admired how we looked, our legs tan and our teeth white with the smiles we would give them. I felt new sensations as I matured into a man, feelings that no one had ever explained to me or told me that I would feel. Excitement and yearning for things that seemed strange, like the way some of the girls would look at me then cock their head at a certain angle, their lips pink and glistening. I had to look away and kick the ball harder just to concentrate. Were these feelings normal? I had seen and heard more than my fair share of things better left unseen, but this was different. I felt strange, like my tongue was too big for my mouth. If my dad were alive, he would have explained these feelings to me and told me that it was normal, that it was okay.

One sultry evening near dusk, many weeks into my second stay in Acapulco, my friends asked me if I wanted to go with them to buy some weed.

"I met a guy who says he has a stash," said my friend, pulling on his backpack. "He lives up in the hills where all the big houses are."

My curiosity piqued, I agreed to go, and our motley crew set out on foot to walk into a section of town I'd never been. The streets got nicer, and cleaner, and big gates with solid concrete fences lined the way. Over the top of the structures, I glimpsed vast blue stretches of rolling ocean. These were the houses of rich locals, tourists who rented, and elements of society that did their business well in the shade.

I stayed in the back of the pack, knowing that my friends trusted people a little too readily. I hadn't yet experimented with drugs, but like all things that come to you in life, it was an inevitable path that pulled me in. My senses were tingling, and my gut was telling me to stay aware.

We arrived at a gate, and my friend looked at a number he had written down and looked back at us and said, "This is it. Let's go in, man."

The gate swung open as he put his hand up to press the button, and we peered around it to see what lay inside. I saw an open, modern structure with many windows facing the ocean. We marveled at the home tucked into the gently rolling hillside, with plants and cool terracotta tile greeting us and pulling us in. A man dressed in khaki shorts and a floral print shirt like was sold in the mercados appeared through the door frame and casually waved us in.

We could smell a sweet, pungent odor as we stepped through the portico and went down a narrow outdoor hallway and onto a patio that faced the ocean. The view was breathtaking, and I sucked in my breath as a near three-sixty view of the bay was seen. *The air is different up here*, I thought, *and it is filtered through nostrils that never in a day have had to breathe the air of the poor folk like us.* I stood straighter and ran a hand through my hair, knowing that a house is just a house and the people in it are just as human as I was.

I turned to see most of my friends moving into the house with the man, who I considered carefully. He spoke Spanish but wasn't fluent. Was he a tourist? A regular in Acapulco? I couldn't yet place him but was wary of his invitation.

They hadn't noticed that I didn't follow them into the house, and I took the opportunity to walk around unnoticed. I explored the exterior of the home and appreciated the concrete, metal, and glass that had come together to perch gently on this precarious foundation. Architecture appealed to me, and I grew excited at seeing how things were built. *Maybe one day I'll be an architect*, I thought, as I ran my hands over the walls' rough texture, warm on my palm.

As I passed through the patio and inside the home, I could smell incense mixed with something else, something sickly sweet. I tiptoed through the open-air living room and into the kitchen. Murmurings came through various doorways, and I had a sense of walking into a womb, an unlit space that was warm and red. I passed a cracked door and could see my circle of friends passing a pipe, their heads thrown back as the drug entered their bloodstream. Their defenses were down, but then I saw the man as well as several others joining them, so I supposed it would be okay—as much as supposing could do. Gentle smoke curled through the doorway, and I breathed it in as I walked away.

I moved down the hallway, which held a long

series of doors and led to an open-ended porch on the end. From one of the rooms, I could hear soft yet sharp moaning seeping out from under the door. My heart started pounding, and I took a deep breath as I put my eye to the keyhole.

Many things you are not prepared for, and the girl I saw lying on the bed, chained to the bed, was one of those things. Her eyes—dark eyes— were filled with the terror of the next flick of the whip held by a very tall white man. His skin pale, almost fluorescent against her skin, grew mottled as he walked the room. She had a gag on her mouth, and as the tip of it fell on her opened legs, the moans—not of ecstasy, but pain—issued out once again.

I stepped back and fell against the wall, then quickly regained composure and headed back the way I had come. Reeling, I went outside for air, gulping it down like oxygen that I couldn't get fast enough inside my chest. I saw a second-level patio and winding stairs leading up to it. I thought maybe I could sit there and process what I had seen, tuck it away where the image would disappear.

I sat on a chair near the railing and laid my cheek on the cool cement. The Pacific undulated beneath me as wave after wave hit the shore in a mesmerizing display of power. While I was lost in my thoughts, a small sound kept flicking the back of my neck; and when I could no longer ignore it, I turned around to see what it was.

There were two doors on the second-level patio, both ornate and trimmed in a wood burnished and lovely. I crept slowly up to one door and gently opened it. The room was dark and no sounds issued from it, so I backed out and went to the second door. The sounds grew louder, a bit more frantic, and I was scared to open the door.

My hand gripped the knob and I turned it to reveal a second dark room. The sounds intensified as I moved into the black velvet and waited for my eyes to adjust to the dark interior. I came to a complete stop and scanned carefully, and when my eyes fell on it, I caught my breath.

In the corner, with a blanket draped over it, sat a large cage. I could hear sounds coming from underneath the blanket, and terror overtook me. Was it an animal? A human? I had to know, and I walked carefully through the room and approached the cage. I lifted a corner of the blanket slowly, with the dread of a million silent goosebumps lifting the hairs on my neck. When the blanket was nearly to the top, the cage rattled fiercely and a face came at me, pushing itself through the bars.

I fell back and onto the bed in horror, as her bulging eyes looked through the bars, attempting to see me in the darkness.

I flicked a light on beside the bed and our eyes met. She was young, maybe my age or younger, and her mouth had a dirty red bandana tied around it. She was naked, sitting on a small woven mat inside the cage, her hands tied behind her back. Hot tears, mixing with the dirt on her face, streamed down and caught themselves in the bandana. I reached one finger in and pulled it down, not knowing what else to do.

"Ayudame, por favor! Please, help me!" she whispered, voice scratchy, as her body convulsed with abject terror.

"Why are you here?" I asked her quickly. "Who brought you?"

She squeezed her eyes shut and opened them once more, and I could see just how young she really was. "They talked to me when I was selling candies on the street," she gulped. "They said I could work for them and clean their house. They said I would earn lots of money." She hung her head against the cage, which bit into her skin and left an imprint. "It was the man with the flower shirt," she said in a tiny voice. "He hurts me."

I looked at her and felt more compassion than I've ever felt—and again saw the evil that this world held underneath a beautiful façade. I looked at her and told her to hold on, to let me see what I could do. My head pounded with indecision. Resolute, I told her I must cover her cage with the blanket just in case, so they would not know I had seen her. She began to cry, a low, heavy sound that entered my brain until it became etched there, ingrained. I looked into her eyes and put my finger to my lips as I flicked off the light.

Should I let her out? What if they catch me and kill me? I was plotting a way as I walked down the second level steps.

The man with the flower shirt came out and pinned me with his stare.

"There you are," he said slowly, deadly even. "We wondered where you were."

Behind him, my friends filed out, their faces blank with the drugs that had entered them. Their help was out of the question, and I was panicked to help her, to set her free. The man was looking at me carefully, his eyes dark with question, and he darted his eyes upward and back down just as quickly. "Don't go anywhere, I'll be right back," he said, as he swiftly went up the steps.

Alarm shot through me, and I knew we had to leave. "Let's go! Right now!" I said, as my friends looked at me blearily, their motions slow and weak. Their eyes questioned me blankly, and I said again, "Hurry! Before he comes down!"

They were mumbling about drugs and things he had for them, things he was going to do for them, but I herded them out into the now dark evening, as quick as they could go, exasperation filling me. We reached the gate, the street, and then descended deep, deeper into the section of town where we stayed.

I looked nervously behind me, filled with dread and relief, but knowing I had failed. I had left her behind and couldn't save her. Her eyes, dark and full of misery, would watch for a rescue that would never come.

I slept fitfully that night; vivid dreams left me dank with sweat when the morning sun lifted my eyelids. My friends were still deep in sleep, but I couldn't get my mind off the sights I had seen. Those eyes, they would never leave me. I still see them today. I wonder if she got away or was swept under the layer of grime that Acapulco hides well.

I got up and walked to a small, cracked mirror and looked into it. I saw a face, young and ready to live, yet with tiny cracks spreading from under my eyes. Lines that showed each moment of a life that was still yet to begin but that had already lived a lifetime.

I packed my small backpack, looked at the others sleeping in a pile on the floor, and closed the door. The sun greeted me in that sleepy, sunlit way as it does in cities of the south, and I walked to the bus stop and caught the first one north.

Acapulco hadn't seen the last of me, but I was on my way back to the States, where my destiny lay.

15.

The river greeted me with its incessant rumbling, and I sat on the bank with the moon glowing above. The silvery light made the river's surface look like ice, with watery fingers that were ready to pull me under as I skimmed across.

Much is made of border crossings. Today, coyotes mean big business with figures upward of ten thousand dollars for someone coming from Mexico or Central/South America. If you're looking to gain passage from across the sea—from any country—raise that figure ten-fold. Most money is raised in a collective effort to arrange safe passage. Most of it can never be paid back. If you want to hear an explanation as to why we cross, then ask the multitude who do it. Sit down and get to know someone who has. Faces, etched with worry and weight, should show you the *why*. Crushing poverty almost never allows success, even by those who try their hardest before they decide to make a border crossing.

Sometimes the question shouldn't be *why* but *what:* What can we do for you? How can we help? The place I now call home has turned inward, dangerously selfish in the "protection" of lands that, in the end, we never really own. Borders are manmade, invisible lines that have been pushed and changed, made unrecognizable by the looting of lands. When you look down from space, all you see are swirling waters and land masses locked together. Always together.

The water in front of me came closer as I stepped toward it, naked save for my underwear. I didn't use coyotes. I didn't need to pay someone for what I could do alone. My body clenched as the freezing water came up to my chin. And I swam, alone and strong on a night of my thirteenth year. And as the water dripped off me on the other side and I put my clothes on, I was focused and sure. My body shuddered, and though I was alone, I also knew what to do.

I hid in the bushes, watched the train, and took off. Running quickly, I grabbed the handle and held on, pulling myself up and bracing against the hot metal. The wheels churned beneath me, but I swiftly slid open the bolt on the door and swung myself in. My breath came in waves, and it took a few seconds to catch my breath.

The second time—and it was like magic. The exhilaration that came over me pulsated in my veins. Sweat and water from the river dried in beads that fell from my hair and spun away into the night air. The stars and low-slung clouds met me with their night song, and I laid my head down and watched them pass. And I slept.

When I arrived in San Antonio, the sun was blasting in the clear blue Texas sky. I slipped out of the car and rolled to the ground, popping back up to brush myself off. I crept in between the train cars and disappeared into the streets.

Those without sense get caught. Standing in one spot for too long or looking confused is what tips people off, especially in areas where there are major modes of transport. In bus terminals and train stations, the key is to blend in. When you walk with confidence and your head up, you aren't hiding anything. Assimilating into the culture is another way I blended in. I dressed neat and sharp, looking like any another Chicano walking to the store or work. I knew several phrases in English and had worked my tongue around the local dialect. I trained myself to incorporate the lilt of their words, watching and listening to friends as they talked. I could pass myself off as a local, because the key to blending in is to actually blend in.

I returned to the fruit market, where the semi-trailers that had housed me for two years remained. The vendors were glad to see me, and my friends as well were elated I had made it back. "Que paso? What happened, and how did you get back?" they wondered, faces eager for a story.

A smile stole across my face, and I said, "I visited my mom and family; then I stayed in Acapulco for several months." I continued to regale them with all that had happened, and their mouths dropped open at the tale. I was good at weaving tales, and my status lifted ever so slightly as well.

"But how did you come back across?" they wondered. Most of them had come with other groups who had used coyotes to cross. I looked at them with a hard stare and said, "I swam. I never use coyotes." They looked incredulous. "Why do I need to give my money to someone just to get me across water?" I said forcefully. "I can do that myself."

As I bedded down in the trailer for the night, I could feel a slight shift in structure, the axis having turned just a few degrees. I had always felt that my confidence turned people toward me. I loved being in control. I questioned where this authority came from: Did I need it because my stepdad had used his so poorly? Did I want to show what being a good leader meant?

Sometimes, the best friends you have come from adversity. When dawn broke and we woke up to start the day, my tentative authority was challenged. I felt a tingle down my spine and knew someone was staring at me—rather, glaring at me. I turned and saw a small group formed around a boy my age, body older than his age like mine, and we looked deep into each other's eyes.

In Spanish, he said, "I will kick your ass. Who do you think you are?" He must have arrived while I was gone and thought he was in charge. His hair was wavy and dark, and he was raging.

"I'm Jorge. Who do you think you are?" I said, circling him, a feeling I hadn't felt before pulsing through me.

"I'm David, and there can't be two leaders here," he said clearly, sharply.

He came at me with fists drawn. I deftly

ducked, and he swung into mid-air. Furious, he turned around again, charging at me. I ducked again. When he was off-balance, I went down with one knee into his back and flipped him over, fists raining down on him. He came back and caught me on the chin, and we were both in the dirt, scrabbling hard. I landed a hard blow to his side, and he doubled over in pain as I pushed him down and sat on top of him, arms pinned behind his head.

He looked at me and I looked him, and our eyes faltered. I got up quickly and stepped back. He sat up, face bruised and torn, and stood slowly. He walked over to me and shook my hand, and we knew that even though I had won the fight, a friendship had been born. Grudging respect for him was borne out of a need to dominate, something we both had.

Friendship can be a precarious thing in situations like ours, but David and I meshed. We were inseparable and ran the fruit market boys like they were our own gang. We were young and alive, with everything to prove. We ran wild, getting tattoos in the middle of the night when a local artist offered them to us. The peacock tattoo sat high on my right arm, he as cocksure and proud as I was.

Days were hot as we worked in the sun, lifting crates of melons, bananas, and tomatoes. Their ripe scent filled my nose as I brought them for the vendors to set out in artful displays. From this little fruit market set in a gravel parking lot, I watched the people come and go, and I wondered about their lives. What were their goals? Were they content to live here in this little part of San Antonio forever? I wanted to go north even farther, to see what I could discover. It seemed I was never content to stay in one place. My life had made me a wanderer.

One particularly hot day, I stripped myself of all but my underwear and plunged under the hose. The guys cat-called me, and I gave them my newly learned, middle-finger gesture. The cool water ran down my back as I soaped myself up to wash the grime of the day away. I was looking forward to walking downtown to see the sights, maybe buy some tacos with my friends. The days were simple, and I didn't see a turn coming soon. Maybe I wish I had.

I felt eyes on me as I turned in the water to wash the soap out of my hair, and when I opened my own eyes, a woman stood fifty feet from me. She was petite, with colored hair burnished like copper, and she didn't take her eyes off me. She had two small children, a boy and a girl, who pranced around her legs, chattering in the way that small children do. I dried myself off, avoiding her gaze, and went to change my clothes.

I had noticed more and more that women were noticing me. My body was changing, and I felt my limbs stretch out into themselves as the days went by. It had gone fast, this change, and I was still easing my way into it, unsure of what it would mean.

After I showered, I spread lotion on my arms and face, and changed into fresh clothes. I walked out of the trailer to see what trouble we could get into for the evening—and found myself face to face with the same woman. She had been waiting for me. She looked me up and down. She was pretty, in a sort of dazed way, her eyes focusing on me with a smile that said much.

"I saw you over here and thought I would say hi," she said softly. "My name is Camila."

I looked at her as her kids ran in circles around us and replied, "My name is Jorge." Not knowing what to say, I looked at the ground and around at the vendors packing up their things for the day.

"If you want, you can come to my house to shower. Any time, really," she said. "Even right now. I can make you supper."

The thought of home-cooked food made my mouth water, and I considered her carefully. She looked sincere, and I said yes.

Once you cross a threshold, you can't turn back, no matter how hard you try. Experiences good and bad stay with you whether you wish them to remain or not. As I walked to Camila's house, I had a strange sense of crossing that invisible line of no return. I shook it off and watched her kids as they pranced around us.

They were both small, Hector, around four years old, and Jacinta, three years old. They looked like little kids do, but with a wistful, far-off look to their eyes. What had life let them see? They craved attention, and though they didn't talk much, they did other things to get me to watch them. Hector made sounds, but couldn't speak words. As I had just met him, I wasn't sure why he couldn't talk. His smile was another story. I put my hand on his head as we walked, and he beamed.

Camila, if I can describe her from memory, was a small—very small—Chicana woman. She was eighteen years old and filled with a stubborn wildness I had never encountered. I was between my thirteenth and fourteenth year, and my experience with women was slim.

As we arrived at her home, an apartment in the housing projects of San Antonio's west side, I entered the blocky, squat building with trepidation. She immediately went to the kitchen and started rattling around pots and pans, looking out at me from behind the cabinets.

I was sitting at the table as a man walked out from another room. He sat down at the table and looked at me and said to her, "Who is this guy?"

She said, "I met him at the market, and he is here to take a shower. I told him he could."

I didn't know who he was and didn't care, but as the air wafted with the smell of homemade tortillas and spices, I could sense something brewing. She set the food down, fragrant and steamy, and we proceeded to eat. Anger stirred in the air and finally he stood up, looked her in the eye, and said, "I'm gone." She smiled and waved at him as he slammed the door shut.

As the food slid down my throat, she looked at me and said, "Don't mind him. We were over from the start."

Alarm bells should have sounded, but when you're young and hungry, they never ring quite as loud as they should. I finished my food, thanked her, and knew it was time to leave.

"No, please don't go. I have some weed we can smoke," she implored.

I hesitated in my cracked plastic chair. Until that point, I hadn't smoked weed very often. Thinking back now, I'm not sure why I stayed, but I did. We settled in on the couch, and she lit up the pipe. I put it to my mouth and let the herb slide down into my lungs, and I blew it out slowly. I had done pot just enough with my friends to know that it made me feel stupid and slow, but tonight it seemed just the right thing to take the edge off the moment. We sat in her living room, the kids tiring themselves out, and let the hazy, dense smoke fill the room. I felt a sense of something I couldn't put my finger on—something new.

She had an open-door policy, and soon we had a ring of friends toking and laughing. Beers were popped open, cold and wet, and I grew comfortable and let myself relax. Evening turned into night, and sleepiness overtook me. Where were her kids? Had she put them to bed? I wondered why I worried about this, her carefree way of parenting pricking at the back of my brain.

I heard her tell me, "You can sleep here in the extra bedroom. Follow me." Her hands motioned to me through my foggy brain, and soon I fell onto a cushion of comfort and heard the door close.

I came up through thick layers of what seemed to be jungle, and I kept pushing back huge, green leaves that were blocking my way. My body felt heavy, and I knew I was dreaming. I was drowning in a thicket of vines that wanted to wrap themselves around me, to choke me. I cried out and felt something slide over my mouth.

My eyes flashed open, and I saw Camila kneeling beside me on the bed, her hand underneath the covers. She was looking at me with eyes dim and feverish, a hunger to the slant of her lips. She had her hand over my mouth, to quiet me, lull me, and as she worked her hands over me, I felt helpless. Surging through my body were quick charges, from the tips of my toes to my neck, and I didn't know how to quell the tide. I watched as she took off her clothes and positioned herself on top of me, never taking her eyes off my face. It occurred to me to say no, but I was here, in this moment, and it felt good. I let myself ride out the swell that was building, and when it was done, she slid off me and lay down beside me.

My arms felt too big for my body, and I sat up to shake off the fuzzy feeling in my head. When I turned to her, she was asleep, curled in a position on her side. I was thirteen, and I didn't know what to feel. I lay down, turned on my side, and stared at the wall as I willed myself to sleep.

I awoke the next morning and Camila was still snoring beside me. I climbed out of the bed quietly and put on my clothes, not knowing for sure how they had been removed the night before.

I looked at her face in the light of day. She was older than me by five years. I found her attractive in an odd sort of way. My mind shuffled through what had happened the night before, and a weird sensation filled me. I tucked it away. I didn't know how to feel.

I slipped out the door and closed it quietly. I needed to leave, to get back to the fruit market. I found her kids in the kitchen, trying to fix themselves breakfast. The clock showed 9:30 A.M. and they stopped their pitter-pattering and looked at me. I could see that they were hungry.

"Do you guys want to go and get something to eat?" I asked. Their eyes grew excited, and they both nodded their heads.

I gathered their hands and walked out the door, looking around for the nearest small eatery. The kids looked up at me, smiling shyly, and I wondered what I had gotten myself into. Growing up hungry was something I couldn't bear to see. I bought several breakfast tacos, and we wandered around for a while, then sat on the front stoop of Camila's apartment.

The kids munched hungrily, and I watched

them as I took one for myself. The steam from the eggs, potatoes, and sausage wrapped up in a flour tortilla wafted into my nose. The south Texas food had been integrated into my food groups.

"Does your mommy always sleep this late?" Hector gravely shook his head yes, and Jacinta stared at me with a blank expression, then smiled and hugged me. I motioned for them to stay there as I went to see if she was awake.

When I entered the bedroom, it was empty. I walked across the hall and peeked into her room. Empty as well. Puzzled, I walked down the short flight of steps and searched every room. She was gone, so I went back outside and sat with the kids until they finished their food.

We came back inside. I settled them on the couch to watch a cartoon and looked around the house. It was chaos everywhere. I picked things up, trying to tidy up, and kept an eye on the kids as they snuggled together.

Twelve noon, and Camila was still nowhere to be found. I rummaged in the refrigerator to find something, once again, for the kids to eat and found nearly bare cupboards. I don't know how she had put together a meal the night before. I scrounged peanut butter and put some on bread and handed it to them, their little faces disappearing behind the big sandwiches.

I need to get out of here, I thought, but couldn't seem to bring myself to leave.

When I had given up hope, in stumbled Camila, her face a terrible mask. I looked at her and she stared blankly at me.

After her marched two women—small, like her—with faces angry and full of rage.

"Who is this?" they asked Camila, as she collapsed onto the couch. The kids gathered around her, clamoring for her attention. She pushed them away, staying inside the haze she had brought into the house.

I looked at her and to the two women, and they said, "We're Camila's sisters, two of them at least." They introduced themselves as Elena and Priscilla, then they turned to her and proceeded to pepper her. They spoke in Spanish, yet with English words sprinkled in, and I could follow.

"What about your babies? Do you care where you end up? They could take them away from you!"

"Stupid little girl. Grow up!"

My nagging feeling, the thing I couldn't put my finger on, had proved me right. Camila was a spray head, a huffer—someone who took a can of spray paint and let the fumes work deep into their brain. Huffing was, and still is, a cheap way to get high. As she lay passed out on the couch, her sisters told me she had been doing it for years. Hector, her four-year-old, couldn't speak because she had done it while pregnant with him.

I looked at Hector, sitting tightly beside his mom on the couch. My senses were tingling as they continued to tell me her story.

"You seem different," Elena said. "Are you staying?"

The nonchalant way they asked, not even knowing me, took me aback. I shook my head and said, "I only just met her last night. I need to get back to my friends. I couldn't leave the kids by themselves." I rose from my chair at the scuffed table and backed over to the door. "Maybe I'll see you again," I said, as I crossed the threshold and breathed the fresh air of the day.

I could hear them across the courtyard, yelling their thanks to me, and I ran down the sidewalk and sprinted as far away as I could get.

I learned a lot living in San Antonio, the way relationships were defined in these circles. When you date someone, they become your "old man" or "old lady," and their relatives become your sister-in-law, brother-in-law, or mother-in-law. Right from the beginning. If you live with them for longer than several months, they say you are "common-law" which is a term for couples who aren't married but live together for long periods of time. The way her sisters had looked at me was an invitation to stay and make her better. To fix her. I was a young teenage boy just waking up to himself. I wasn't ready to raise kids or be a parent.

I didn't know if I was ready for that kind of responsibility.

My friends grilled me when I got back to the trailers and laughed when I told them what had happened. "We've seen her around," they said. "She's been coming around here a lot." I also saw a twinge of jealousy in their eyes. We were all getting older and conscious of who we were.

My friend David, especially, seemed upset by what had happened. "Why did you go with her?" he asked, not hesitating to show his anger.

"Why do you care? It's not like it meant anything," I said to him, looking him directly in the eye. He was jealous. Lots of girls had been looking at me, and even though we had a tight friendship, competition is a thing between friends—especially ones who vie for leadership.

I didn't think of her after that day and went about my minutes the way I always had. Until she showed up several days afterward, looking for me. I flinched when I heard her call my name.

"Jorge! There you are!" she said, the hope in

her voice unmistakable. I turned to look at her, sweat dripping off my back, and closed the distance to where she stood. "Hi," she said. "I'm sorry for what happened. I really want you to come and live in my house. I'll rent you the room you stayed in." Her face held a look of innocence that I could see right through. What did she want with me? I wasn't looking for anything except to take care of myself. I could see David watching me out of the corner of my eye.

"I'll think about it," I said, wiping my brow. "I'll let you know."

She smiled, and I felt a small tug—not of love, but of something—and watched her turn around. She looked back and said, "The kids really liked you. I do, too." With that she continued down the street until I couldn't see her anymore.

Every day after that she came by, bringing me different things. There were homemade tortillas filled with eggs, chorizo, and potatoes, or handmade tamales. She was relentless in her pursuit of me, and she connected that with my stomach and being away from home. Our difference in age never came up. Every time, I thanked her and she left, leaving me to my own decision. Sifting through my thoughts, I reminisced on all the places I had ever stayed. I had slept on the street, in a train car, on the floor in houses, and in a semi-trailer. How bad would it be to rent from her and have a bed to sleep in? I knew there would be a price to pay, as I remembered the eyes of those kids, as well as hers in the dark of night.

The next day when she came around, I told her I would rent the room. We agreed on a price, and the day after, I carried my small bag of things into the spare bedroom. I lined up my small bottles of cologne on the shelves and hung up my clothes in the closet.

What was I agreeing to? Was it more than just renting a room?

16.

Something in me was changing, and I was becoming a person that I didn't recognize. Girls noticed me, and the older I got, the more I was drawn to them. I saw the way they looked at me, smiling at every turn I made. I had grown up without being taught about the opposite sex, no one telling me how it was to feel these feelings.

When Camila had sex with me on that first night, it had opened a door that I couldn't close. The night after I moved in with her, I left the house and headed down to a dance they were holding on Market Square. I needed to breathe my own air. I had become accustomed to it. I was a good dancer. I saw my friends arrive and nodded to them from across the dance floor. David was dressed up, with his hair slicked back, and our grins were simultaneous.

Swinging myself into the center of crowd, I offered my hand to a girl and twirled her around as the music pumped out Norteño. The music swelled high and I held her close, not knowing who she was. It didn't matter. These dances were for losing your inhibitions and feeling another person in your arms alive and smiling. I felt small twinges of doubt, having moved in with Camila. I moved my arms around and swung the dark-haired girl forward and back again, and we smiled as the movement caused us to feel the heat between our young bodies.

As we twirled to the two-step, I heard a commotion from the back of the dance floor. I could hear yelling and thought a fight had broken out—but no, it wasn't a fight. I was horrified to see that Camila had followed me, and she was screaming her way toward me, yelling obscenities as she came. I could see her sister and her brother, Paul, behind her.

I stopped dancing and walked away from the square and she came at me.

"Why are you here dancing with other girls? Why?" she screamed. "I thought we were together?" Her face was pinched into a mask of ugliness, and I could see that she was high.

"I'm only renting a room from you," I said as calmly as I could manage.

She began screaming and crying, and I grabbed her by the arm and pulled her onto the sidewalk. In these short few days, her brother and sisters considered me part of the family. They knew I was looking out for her and wanted me for their brother-in-law. At least, that's what they called me.

"Why did you let her come here?" I asked them, for lack of anything better to say.

"We couldn't stop her. She went crazy when she woke up and you weren't there," they said.

"She left the kids with Priscilla and started walking over here. We followed her."

Camila was ranting and raging as she sat down on the sidewalk, hair plastered to her face from the tears. We went home, and I put her to bed. She looked at me and said, "Please don't leave me. Please." I walked out and went to my room. I stared at the ceiling, my hands like a weight behind my neck.

The bus banged and tore around curves, depositing me in my town in central Mexico once again. I had needed to get back to Mexico again, and I wanted to make another trip to Oaxaca, and have Chucho go with me. I always left him behind to stay with the family. I felt like the prodigal son, taking the fatted calf while he got scraps, and an adventure was in order.

After visiting for a few days, I took my brother aside and said, "We're going to Oaxaca. Pack a bag!"

He looked at me sideways and a slow grin started to form, yet I could see the hesitation. He had never been away from home, never tried to leave. I could see him struggling to decide whether he should, and finally I threw some clothes in a bag and told him we were leaving in the morning.

"What about Mom and Dad?" he said. "What will they say?"

I laughed and looked at him, always feeling like the older brother. "Carnal, we're not going to tell them."

As the morning fog lifted off the dry scrub around the house, we slipped away and onto a bus bound for Oaxaca. I had money stuck away, always money in my pockets, and the excitement grew, the closer we got.

But excitement turned to hesitancy, and I could see in his face that he was uneasy. When we got off the bus, I took him to all the spots I had been. We ate at the taco stands and markets I knew. The city was alive, and we went to the square at night and watched the revelers dance until dark. I wanted him to see and understand where I'd been all those years; to get a taste of my life being lost. But when night fell, I saw fear wash across his face as we bedded down on the hard streets. For as little as he had ever had in his life, I could see that he was afraid.

Several of my friends were with us, and I asked them if our other friend still had a room he stayed in. Finding it in the darkest of city nights, I asked if my brother could sleep inside for the night. He agreed, kindred souls always sticking together, and I went back out to sleep on the ground.

I came back for Chucho when dawn broke, and for several more days we prowled the cobblestone streets of the city. But I could see he was ready to go home; his eyes gave him away.

We boarded a bus north, where I left him. I loved my brother so much, but he wasn't meant to be away from home, from Mom and Dad. My heart ached for what I felt I had done to him, for how I had made him afraid to leave my parents' side. He deserved so much more than what life had given him so far.

As leaves blow from trees in the fall, so the days moved on. I was well into fourteen and had stayed at Camila's house off and on, coming and going as I pleased. She always wanted more than I could give. She had kids and wanted to sit at home and smoke; my head was blowing in the wind, ready for adventure, to see different spaces. She didn't have a job outside the home, and I would give her extra money to make sure her kids were fed. It was a cycle I wasn't sure I liked.

She would disappear for days, coming back high, face littered with paint splotches. Some days I would go looking for her, after the kids had fallen asleep, and she would be underneath bridges or down in the huge drainage ditches that ran through the city. She was always with a bag to her mouth, breathing in and out, the fumes turning her brain to mush. I dragged her back to the apartment and left her on the couch.

Had she seen in me someone to take care of her? I had dragged my dad home one too many times off the street, stinking of urine and stale alcohol. I didn't want to do it again.

I decided to go home to Mexico yet again for my fifteenth birthday. My frequent visits helped me to know that I still had roots and a place in the world that knew me. I told Camila I was leaving for a few months, and her face gave away her emotions. This was nothing new, and I packed my bag as she raved on and on about me leaving her.

I looked at her and said, "I'm going for a couple months. I'll be back."

The kids hugged my legs as I walked out the door. In the short time I lived there, I had been more of a father to them than their own dad. I left money for her on the table and told her to use it for the kids, as she pocketed it and turned away, face red and mottled. I don't know why I cared, but when I looked at their faces, I saw myself. Though they had a mom, I saw them alone, having to face each day on their own.

My trip by bus was uneventful, and when I arrived, I saw that another face had been added to our family. We totaled five now; seven, if you count my brother and my sister who died. My mom was so happy to see me, and even though she looked tired, she was still beautiful to me.

Whenever I visited, my dad made himself scarce. He was afraid of me as I grew older and stronger each time I returned. He tried to assert himself at times and places, but I wouldn't stand for it anymore.

Once, when one of my extended uncles was at the house drinking with my dad, my uncle started arguing with me. He was a mean man whose life had turned him bitter. He had had a wife and a child in the United States and they had left him, leaving him to return empty-handed and angry. He married my aunt and beat her mercilessly.

When the argument started, I rose up out of my chair, every beating my stepdad had ever given me pounding a drum inside my heart, and I started hitting him. Something took over me and I couldn't stop until my uncle was lying on the ground defeated. My dad stared at me, seeing his own demon that he had created in me. It was the first time I saw him show fear, a wanting to disappear from my presence.

My mom came out of her shell when I came home. In these moments, I could find her, draw her out, and try to talk to her about all the emotions we both still held. She would talk for a time, then her eyes would glaze over, and I knew I had lost her. Considering all these years with my stepdad, never being able to talk about the family she had lost, never a day without anger and punches—the forgetfulness was not out of the ordinary. But unlike me, she had willed herself to forget. I never would.

By this time, Chucho had met a girl whose name was Malena. Chucho had done his fair share of stepping out and attending dances. He was a favorite in the town, with his slicked back hair and shiny teeth. They all said he looked like Elvis. Plenty of girls wanted to be with him, but he was smitten with Malena. He looked happy, happier than I'd seen him.

After I went back to San Antonio, I would find out that they had run away to be together. Mexican parents, as I mentioned before, don't make it easy to be together. In the circle of our small town, there is always fussing over whether this or that family is good enough, and while the bickering goes on, the couple runs away to be together. When they come back, it's too late. The rituals of dating in Mexico are unique as every sunset.

I hid many facts from my mom—like smoking weed and dating girls. I pretended to be the little boy she had lost, the one who whenever she looked at him would be the one she had found. I shouldn't have let this delicate dance continue, but I was good at pretending.

The fact remained, though, that when I visited, even though I was there for only a short time, girls noticed me. They were furtive in their glances and looks because Mexican girls were good at being secretive. I banished Camila from my mind and flirted back. I had grown comfortable with women and making them feel special. I knew the tone of my voice and the softness or hardness with which I spoke made them laugh. It was a power I needed to be careful with. I often wondered if my real dad had had the same power, and in the end, it had killed him.

I met a girl during this time named Xochitl, and I thought she was beautiful. She was petite, with dark, piercing eyes. Both of us fifteen, we were inseparable in the time I was there. I met her in town, and we would sit and hold hands, kissing in corners, as happens in most public places. With my hands and lips, I sold her on promises of love.

I believed that I needed to respect my mom and not bring trouble to her, so a girl never graced the entrance of my house. My mom was jealous of my time, and if I was only there for a short time, why should I upset her? I believe she saw my dad when she looked at me: my frame, the turn of my jaw, it was him. There was no mistaking that I belonged to him, and his presence still lingered in my every move. This was why my stepdad couldn't stand me. For that reason alone, I never brought girls home to meet my mom.

My cousin Gregorio—Gorio for short—was stout and solid and my closest cousin, a brother, really. He was the kind of cousin that you could tell anything to and get in the most trouble with. Whenever I came home, we were thick as thieves. On one of my trips back, we were doing our normal routine, hanging out in San Juan, flirting with girls, and getting into trouble. Gorio thought stealing a pellet rifle would be funny, and as we ran down the alley with it, we saw his dad and my stepdad standing together near the market. They both turned their heads and locked eyes with us. We'd been caught.

We took off like a shot, and instead of going

home, we took a bus into Mexico City. There we switched buses to one going to Acapulco. Gorio was terrified of getting into trouble, and I was always up for an adventure. When we arrived in the city six hours later, we were tired and dirty but feeling alive. We spent several days bumming around. We stealthily stole some clothes off the mounds of clothing in the market and found a way to bottle baby oil in used, empty Búfalo salsa bottles to sell to tourists for tanning. We feasted on cheap seafood and tacos, gorging ourselves with the money we'd made bilking them.

One day we went swimming in the ocean to cool off, leaving our clothes on the sand. When we came back a man was waiting for us where our clothes had been. He said he'd give them back if we gave him money. We'd spent it all on food and had nothing. We tiptoed through the hot streets in our underwear, stealing shorts and shirts from unsuspecting vendors.

We left Acapulco, hitchhiking to Oaxaca City where we found day work in a bakery and a pharmacy. Gorio's parents had been looking for him, and a cousin he had in Oaxaca spotted us and told his parents. They sent money for a train ride home, and we never heard the end of it.

I was changing. I could feel the sudden wind blow in between the two personas of my life. In Texas, I was Jorge, fearless leader of whatever group I was in. That Jorge smoked and ran wild, bringing all who challenged him under his control. In Mexico with my family, I was Toño. I was the boy who had been lost, and the one who brought money, clothing, and food to my little brothers and my sister. I was the one they looked up to, a father figure, and I had seamlessly become that person, without effort. I was the good son, the one who never caused problems, and who made everything better. I had become larger than life in their minds.

At fifteen in Texas, I was the one who lived with an older woman and her kids, who paid rent to her and helped her buy food. I was also the one who had sex with her and closed my eyes as it happened, not sure why my body betrayed my feelings. In Mexico, I was the one who promised sweet nothings in the ears of girls who believed that I would return to them.

I was full of goodness and chaos, and my two sides were about to explode into a person I wasn't sure I knew.

The water hit me hard in the face, freezing as always, and I swam a smooth stroke to the other side of the river. I could hear mumblings and incoherent voices coming from either side. Downriver, I could see the swirling lights of Immigration vans, gathering up people who had come to seek more, their journey ended before it could even begin. I climbed out and quickly put my clothes on, beat a path to the brush, and ran for the tracks.

To people who have everything, my journeys might seem dangerous, foolish. The first time I crossed, I did it for the adventure; now, I did it to make something of myself.

Often, Americans will say, "If you love your country so much, why do you leave and invade our country?" *Invade* is a loaded word, so I smile and shake my head. People will leave a place, no matter how much they love it, if it means creating opportunity, giving the family a chance to step out of poverty, a refuge for those displaced by violence from their government or family. The place of your birth is sacred, whether you stay there or seek new lands. Though we always remember our homeland, the rhythms of daily life, the way its flavors burst on your tongue, we embrace the new one we've entered. Why do so many of us, including me at that time, come undocumented? We come because the doors to the United States are closed to us, never having been given the chance to try.

Americans lose sight of the opportunities they have. There are incredible paths to success available to them, but when this advantage is not used, complacency can set in. Many complain and say, "When will my time come? It's my turn to succeed," and in the same breath do nothing about it. When people yearn to enter the United States, they seek the opportunity, and they don't waste time complaining—they start doing.

The United States has become an insular society, open only to people who can show they have money. It has lost sight of the worth immigrants bring, and especially in recent years the blinders have grown thicker and higher. Words, when used to tear down and demonize others, build the highest of walls because of fear. As for me, I made my own future.

I could hear the train whistle and saw the black hulk snake toward me. I gathered my bag, hit the ground running, and silently braved the churning wheels. Catching the latch and swinging it open, I entered the train car and watched the south Texas landscape fly by. I could smell the strange scent of change on the breeze.

I awoke in the morning with a startling alertness, and knew things were going to change.

San Antonio had never been my stopping point—I wanted to see all of America. Having arrived back late at night, I had not gone to Camila's and instead went to the fruit market. I looked around me at the sleeping forms and whistled sharply, as heads popped up, protesting the early wake-up.

"If anyone wants to come along, I'm heading north on the train," I said, voice echoing. "I'm leaving tonight."

I could hear everyone babbling, not sure what to make of the proposition. I went outside and stepped under the cold stream of water. My hair lathered into a soapy mess, and as I washed it out, my soul felt cleansed. Life could feel like an episode of the Twilight Zone, a rush in the moment, invincibility, a longing for clarity. Not pouncing on the moment can let fear creep in.

This is the way to go, I said to myself. *This is it.*

17.

Night was crisp and clear as the black velvet sky enveloped our entrance into the train yard. Several of my friends followed me, excited for new adventures to the mundane every day. My chest felt clearer, the pot smoke slowly siphoning out as I breathed in the air.

I gathered everyone around and looked them in the eye and said, "Follow my mark. When the train starts moving, do not run." I explained to them about waiting as it stopped and started, the conductor trying to weed out those who tried to jump it. "You have to be smarter than them," I said, as the thrill of the night filled me.

We crouched behind several other cars, and I singled out the train I knew to be headed north. Instinct coursed through me, and as the train stopped and started several times, I waited, nerves jangling like electricity through me. Then I saw the train moving and picking up speed.

I took off. The wind brushed past my face and I could hear the pounding of feet behind me, slightly uncertain yet following without doubt. I leapt off my feet and hung on tightly to the iron bars, willing myself up to the handles that allowed me to grab them, like welcoming hands. I opened the door and swung myself in.

Looking back, I saw my friends coming fast, and one by one they jumped in. We were four young punks trying to find ourselves in a big world not quite big enough to contain us. I motioned for everyone to find a seat behind the stacks inside the cars.

As the motion of the train lulled us to sleep, thoughts of David, who had stayed behind, and

Camila filled me. I knew I was juggling too many balls at a time—girlfriends in Mexico, girls here. I needed to figure out a way to manage it all without drowning.

I was in a dark place, shivering violently, as men in dark suits danced around me in a circle. They were poking at me, prodding me, and I couldn't move, or I would break into a million pieces. My eyes shot open, and I realized I was dreaming.

The cold had been real. Sometime overnight, the temperature had dropped to near freezing, and our body temperatures along with it. I could see my friends in a huddle, gathered for warmth, miserable, as the train chugged into weather I had not experienced before. Were we still in Texas? I peeked outside, and a bright, silvery moon shone on vast plains. We had to still be here, but this cold, oh the cold, made my body ache. None of us had coats, the warmth long since leaving our bodies. I looked around, desperate to find something for protection.

The entire car was filled to the brim with unopened boxes. I ripped into one, hoping to find something—anything—and when I saw that they were chock full of clothing, my heart did a little jump. Digging down in, I could see that it wasn't just any clothing; it was brand-name clothing. The good stuff. The things we couldn't afford to buy in stores. My friends grabbed what they could and put it on over their clothing to banish the chill.

I went around the car, checking each box for its contents. When I was done, a plan had hatched in my brain. The crazy ideas I had. I was always looking for the next way to succeed, always. This, however, was a no-brainer. I loved stories of the Old West—the Lone Ranger, Aguila Solitaria, and train robbers who blazed their way to glory. I don't know about glory, but I loved a good Billy the Kid tale. I hadn't named myself after Jorge Rivero, a famous actor in cowboy movies, for nothing. These boxes were a gold mine, shipping everyday across this vast nation, and they were ripe for the picking. This was the way to make money, and I was going to be the leader. Trains, once again, were about to be a major player in the story of my life.

I knew that it was too cold to continue, so when the train slowed down at the next stop, we jumped off. But we had been seen, and we were so cold that officials had taken us into custody. We had made it to Memphis, Tennessee. We sat under blankets in the police car for quite some time, and very soon we were on a train back to Texas. They had simply turned us around and sent us home. My thoughts were forming rapidly with logistics and ways to make my new plan happen. I had found the tip of an iceberg when I opened that first box. I was about to send it all into overdrive. My friends looked at me like I was crazy, but I knew that I wasn't.

When we arrived back at the trailers, everyone

wondered why we had come back. After explaining about the cold, plus getting caught and released, I proceeded to lay out the plan. Everyone stared at me, eyes shifting warily to each other, as I continued to talk and plan.

"I don't care whether you're with me or not," I said. "But if you are, there's no going back. I want you all in or not." I could sense a shift in the group and knew the ones who would follow.

As we put our heads into heavy conversation, the plan took shape. A group of us would jump the train and wait to start tossing the boxes until we were out in the plains. The second group would steal however many cars we needed and meet at a designated spot. They would pick up the boxes and us after we had jumped off the train, and we would split—no one the wiser. Selling the goods would take a bit more planning. I had a friend from San Antonio who had connections, a place that maybe—just maybe—would take the stolen goods. Everything hinged on it. My fifteen-year-old mind churned as we lit a joint and passed it around the group. I took a hit and let the drug run through my lungs. A wave of calm slowly pervaded me, and I knew that everything would be all right.

Each day we pulled the plan tighter and tighter until it seemed foolproof. Satisfied, I headed to the nearest park and climbed to the top of the monkey bars. I liked to come here to think, and I looked around, surveying my kingdom. I had learned that people would follow me, almost blindly. I felt strong and calm. I didn't know what my younger self had hoped for in life. A warm bed? A home to call my own? Or maybe a life without someone hitting me? Small, tiny wishes tucked away for the future still danced in my brain. They were never far from sight, and I held onto them as I stepped into things—right or wrong—that were inevitable.

I looked down, as the sun began to set and saw someone walking toward me. I could see it was a woman, and as she came closer, I saw that it was Camila. I sighed and turned my head, watching several cars pass by, and when I turned back, she was beneath me.

"Will you come home with me? I want to make you supper," she said, her face with dark patches that circled her eyes. She looked gaunt and sickly, and I wondered how her kids were and how many spray cans she had used that day.

"How are Hector and Jacinta?" I asked, as she kicked a piece of gravel beneath her shoe.

"They're fine—at my sister's house right now," she muttered. "I'm trying to pull myself together." I knew she was anything but together, but a tiny shard of compassion welled up in me. I looked at her and jumped off the monkey bars.

"Let's go," I said, taking her hand. We walked to her house where warm tortillas and carne guisada waited. It was savory as it hit my belly, and as we walked up to her room, I conceded that part of my life secmed destined to have her in it.

The train rushed below me as I stood on the

overpass. I could feel each car and its heavy load lumber over the tracks, its burden weighing it down as it picked up speed. I stepped over the side of the bridge and waited, counting cars as they whooshed underneath me, rattling the supports. I jumped, and the train spiraled toward me as I slammed and rolled onto the top of the car. My shoulder felt split in half.

I sensed the others jump and nearly roll off the top. I looked at them and swung down the side, then jimmied my way to the door. Once it was open, everyone dropped down and slipped inside, like spirits gliding through the night.

We went to work, each one with a task to do. We split each box open, checking inside to make sure we got the good stuff. There were boxes of sporting goods—sweatshirts, shoes, and sweats—that were stacked by the door, ready to make a journey into the night. Other boxes contained watches that gleamed gold and silver, and others held designer clothing intended for high-end stores.

I stepped out and worked my way down to the other cars, examining the contents until we were satisfied that we had the best merchandise. We didn't want to miss anything, so thoroughness was our friend as the sky turned the blackest shade of midnight.

How did I know what to do? I never questioned myself, I just did what I came to do and kept on doing it. Inside me was a hunger for more, the thrill of the chase, and I would not be stopped.

I knew the designated place to drop was fast approaching. We had watched the train schedules and knew when they stopped and started. Being on time was imperative to success—and I would not fail.

I hung out the side and whistled. Heads were stuck outside the train as we sped down the tracks, and when I dropped my hand, boxes flew into the air. Poetic, almost, as they ascended into the night sky and fell violently to the ground.

When it was done and the train was rolling

into its stop, we tumbled out and onto the scrub, allowing the rocks to embrace us with minimal damage. Scrambling into the bushes, we began the dark trek back to where the boxes lay and where the stolen cars should be. We had had no communication with our friends who were on car duty. I could only hope that they had done just as well as we had.

Covered in soot, we could see headlights coming toward us, and they flashed quickly. I knew it was them. They had already loaded the boxes, and we climbed in and drove off before we were spotted. My mind was filled, and I looked back to survey my crew. Head to toe dirty, but smiles all around.

We didn't stop until we reached San Antonio, sleeping bodies draped over the backseat like crumpled blankets. We were a pack of young kids, not quite old enough to drive, yet filing slowly down a dark street to unload our stolen goods. I dropped most everyone off and told them to go home. We would come back later.

I continued with only the drivers and my friend who had the connection until we reached a small alley. The night weighed heavy, and I knew the next step would be the most precarious one. A light glowed underneath a door covered in graffiti and riddled with scratches. I gave the driver a look to stay there, to keep his head down, and be silent. Quietly, we walked up to the door and knocked. My goal was to remain silent but aware. My heart pulsed within me. I knew we could be killed just for knocking.

The door cracked, letting shabby light spill onto the rough concrete. "Que quieres? What do you want?" a pair of lips said. His hair was black and slicked back with pomade, one curl resting against his cheek.

"We've got some stuff to sell," my friend said, as I stood stock still. We were putting it all on the line, taking the biggest risk of our lives.

The door creaked open further. "What do you have?"

"Stuff from the train. Good stuff," my friend

said, keeping his voice to a deep, steady monotone.

I could see him sizing us up, but I didn't turn away and looked him straight in the eye.

"Show me," he said.

We turned around and I saw the driver straighten up in his seat. We led him to the back of all three cars and opened each trunk. The piles and piles of goods lay neatly stacked in boxes, ready to be taken. He nodded his head and with no expression on his face told us to follow him back in. I saw figures come from a door and begin to unload the trunks, and I hesitated as the whole load of goods disappeared before we received any payment.

"Here's what I can do for you," he said. "Half in cash, and half in product."

My eye twitched slightly, but my friend kept his face a mask. "I want all cash," he said, knowing he meant to pay us in drugs.

"I can't do it," he said solidly. My heart pounded, and I knew it was make or break, right now, and if I wanted to do business with him, we would have to give a little.

"Okay, seventy-five percent cash, twenty-five percent product," my friend said, a little harsher than needed.

His eyes sparked and he retorted, "Sixty/forty. That's it."

My friend stuck his hand out and the deal was struck. I didn't know exactly how much cash I was getting, but I had won a hard bargain nonetheless. A wad of cash appeared; he licked his fingers and shoved a huge pile toward us. We didn't have a bag, but he found a discarded paper one and I stuffed the cash in quickly before the deal could be changed.

Another bag was thrust toward us, and as I peered inside, I knew that this would change everything. Fluffy and white, the powder lay deep inside. I looked at him and walked out the door, my friend making small talk as he backed away, and I knew that whatever I would bring, he would buy.

We got in the cars and drove slowly away, ditching them on a side street, and walked the quiet streets so silent in the dead of night. My friend and I parted ways and I thanked him for getting me in. My hands were full of money and drugs.

Everyone was sleeping when we arrived back at the trailers. As my head hit the pillow, I stared up at the ceiling as the night played out before me like a silent film—until sleep hit me like a brick to the head.

I was flush with coke and money. In all the years I had lived on the streets and in rundown houses with my mom, my dream was to make it, to have enough money that we would no longer have to worry about food or clothing. I knew that I couldn't just pray and expect miracles as I had when I was small; I needed to go and get the job done. When the door opens you strike, because it's all wrong if you think the work will be done for you.

I divided somewhere around 15K among my

crew, as well as loading their pockets with drugs. I didn't care what they did with it. I looked at the money in my hands and felt a deep hunger inside me to do more. My guys would do whatever I asked.

A few of us had tried cocaine before, but not all. Here before us were piles of white powder, glistening and slippery. I didn't want to sell it; I knew that. We had scored such a big amount of money that none of us wanted to do anything but celebrate.

I poured some of the coke out onto the table we had, formed several jagged lines, and looked at it. I didn't know what would happen, but I felt like the king of a very big world. I put my nose down and snorted the entire line and threw my head back. My friends all looked at me in anticipation and soon followed with their own lines.

My body tensed, and a feeling I had never felt before coursed through me. I felt alive, like I could run forever. Euphoria spread throughout each cell of my limbs. This powder, so white like clouds slipping through my fingers, was going to be my rush as well as my kryptonite. I felt invincible.

I started to snort lines each time we went back to hit the train. I felt superhuman; every aspect of the plans was in my control. This world had encompassed me thoroughly—especially when the cocaine was jolting through my blood, hot and light. I would jump the train and ride for miles underneath the cars, the metal, hot and greasy, tightly held by my hands that felt stronger than the strongest man. When I swung myself up inside the train cars, the drugs held me, cradled me, my brain held tight by a needed vise grip. It had given me vision. The night sky was brilliant with stars each time we filled the stolen cars with boxes and boxes of top-of-the-line goods. No one could catch us. We were untouchable, and the money poured in.

In between train outings, I continued my off-

and-on relationship with Camila. Some nights were lonely. She would find me and beg me to come to her house. Sometimes I showed up and there would be men sprawled all over the living room, high on the fumes of a mountain of spray cans. Brown paper bags littered the floor, and the smell inside the house would be nearly intolerable.

Her kids would be huddled inside on a chair, watching whatever the TV could pick up on the antenna. Fuzzy programs of *Sesame Street* and *Mister Rogers' Neighborhood* would come through, and I would ask them if they were hungry. Their mom oblivious and in her own world, we would walk to the local store and buy bread, meat, and cheese for sandwiches. I would sit with them at the old table she had, cracked placemats holding triangles of bologna and cheese, and talk to them while they swallowed large bites their small mouths could barely swallow. I could see my brothers and my sister in them, and their need drew me in.

I couldn't be their mom, though, and she seemed incapable of helping herself. I would sleep with her, but I didn't feel good afterward. Was I searching for solace for myself? After several days, I would leave, and I'd feel a thousand-pound weight lifted off my shoulders.

The trailers at the fruit market were awash with new arrivals and regulars. Some of us came and went, but I kept my base there. I wanted to be mobile, not tied down to any one place in case I needed to get out quick.

18.

David and I were thicker than ever as we worked the trains together and after much jostling for leadership, we had settled into a good friendship. He was from Monterrey and wanted to go home for a visit.

"Will you come with me?" he asked one evening, the cocaine washing over us like a frigid stream of water.

Alive and tingling, I said, "When do we leave?"

The next morning, we set off on a bus that took us right through the border and straight down to

Monterrey, which was a couple of hours into Mexico. We were kindred spirits, David and I, with similar tastes in women and an embedded streak of competition. We were young and cocky. I wanted everything the world could give me, and as I slipped further into hedonistic behaviors, I was full of clarity.

I had grown to near maturity, or at least what I thought was maturity, and girls wouldn't leave me alone. I was aloof, never seeking them, yet they found me wherever I went. David and I made it into a game, to see how many we could make out with.

David had friends in La Tropa Colombia, a band very popular at that time. Their music swelled as we arrived at a local neighborhood dance. As the music rose in pitch and fever, we swirled the girls around the dance floor. My hips ground and shook, taking willing arms in breathless circles, swinging them out, then back toward me and my waiting arms. They would lean in for wet kisses as we twirled them away to the next person waiting in line.

I was callous and I knew I was a player. I felt torn in half, two different people, one capable of compassion and love, and one who didn't give a shit. I was reckless with my emotions and had created a hard, impenetrable shell that couldn't be cracked. Only on occasion did I let a sliver of light in. I was mostly heartless, leaving bruised hearts behind. So many people had come and gone in my life that I had learned not to care.

Now, with the cocaine running rampant through me, I had something else that helped me not to care. I had money—lots of it—and was careening into dangerous territory. And I opened my mouth to swallow it all.

After staying with David and meeting his family, I left him in Monterrey to visit my own family. Arriving home, I surveyed the house with an eye to detail. My family had moved—three times, to be exact. They went from the white house to a small rental in town and from there to a corner lot in a previously undeveloped part of

Maquixco. I wanted to buy them a piece of land to build a house on. I needed to do this. But my stepdad—how I hated every single word that came out of his mouth. Building my mom a house would allow me to know that I had helped her. Why did I try? I would ask you the same question—do you leave your family to perish? To starve? Even when the most hateful things happen to you, they are still your family.

When I arrived at the corner lot, they were living in a lean-to. The little kids ran to me as my mom was preparing food in the corner, under a tarp hanging from pieces of wood and dripping with water.

I had been sending money to my cousin—my dad couldn't be trusted to collect it—and my cousin would then deliver it to my family. My mom didn't have an I.D. and couldn't sign for the money, so this was the next best option. I believed if I sent money, building a house would be accomplished. These were the instructions I had sent as the money I was making began to grow.

But it hadn't happened.

I set aside my angry thoughts about the house. If I was being truthful, Xochitl was the one I thought about most. Sometimes, when falling asleep at night, my heart grew tender and I thought that maybe we would marry, that she would always wait for me.

After days of wild and unchecked behavior, I showered and applied aftershave. I combed my hair just so, perfect feathered waves, and smiled in the mirror.

"I'll see you later, Ma!" I said. I made my way to Xochitl's house, in a village close to the pyramids, its rough streets washed clean from afternoon rains. I knocked on the door, not a single worry in my head.

Her mom answered, and the surprise on her face should have tipped me off.

"Hi, how are you?" I beamed. "Is Xochi here?"

Not missing a beat, she invited me in, as we

must in Mexico when visitors are at the door. We rounded the door into the dining room, and I recognized that the table was full of people. I saw Xochi in her chair, shock on her face.

Her brother came over quickly to greet me. He gave me a hug, and as he did, I glanced around the table at several unfamiliar faces.

"I want to introduce you to Manuel, Xochi's husband," he said, with his hand firmly planted in the center of my back. All the blood rushed to my face, and for the first time I was speechless.

"Sit down," her mom said, setting a plate of food in front of me. In all the times I had revered Mexico for its hospitality, I wished at this moment that decorum could fly out the window and me along with it. I choked down the food, tasteless on my tongue, and nodded my head as awkward small talk was made.

When I had eaten and passed the amount of time deemed respectful, I excused myself and said I needed to go. Xochitl looked at me from underneath her eyelids, and I learned at that moment that the whole world didn't revolve around what I wanted. It didn't revolve around me. I said goodbye, and she got up along with her husband. Her belly was big, and I turned away.

Her brother walked out with me, and his eyes said how sorry he was, and I fled. The street swallowed me as I walked back into town to sit in the square and think about what had just happened. But it wasn't long before I heard the pulsing songs of a dance happening down the street, and soon I was swaying in the arms of someone new, if just for the night. I had learned to let people disappear in the past as quickly as they came.

Returning to San Antonio, I cast Xochi aside in my mind, and we kept ourselves to a tight schedule. My nose was awash in powder, and it clung to my every pore—inside and out. It entered my every cell. Cocaine gives you a beguiling euphoria and the feeling that everything you set out to do is yours. The drugs were a means to an end, and I used that power, trying not to let it use me. This friend helped me be ten times the achiever I already was. I let its power spread through me nightly. And as I allowed it to rush in, I threw my head back and felt it.

Somewhere in this blur, acid was introduced; and soon I was on a cocktail of smoking weed during the day, snorting cocaine at night, and adding a pop of acid to make things even headier. Yet I was in control. My body and mind felt invincible.

Our once-a-week train schedule went as follows: Meet at the train yard, jump on, wait until the train was out of the city, then go through every car until we find the best merchandise. Throw merchandise out at the designated place, jump off, meet the others who have the stolen cars waiting. More than once a week, and carelessness would set in. I wanted a rigid schedule that would allow us to remain elusive. We would go on different nights, never the same, and like clockwork the deed would be done.

Money, large stacks of cash that with pinpoint precision were handed to me each week, made my street cred grow. I had caught the eye and attention of those higher up in the business, and I was tending that fragile, promising thread. I taught my guys how to discern between the good stuff and the best stuff. I brought my buyers high-end things and was paid well for it. I learned to negotiate for more without making enemies. The pipeline was laid, and I made sure it was pumped full. I was delivering the goods on my own now, and with a nod I would disappear from those back alleys, a little richer each time.

Mexico was never far from our minds, and we would talk of it incessantly, longing for the food and familiar faces. It was comfort more than anything else that we missed. For me, it seemed, comfort had been long gone from my life. Even when I returned to Mexico, there was no ounce of comfort for me. I looked happy on the outside, but the toughness had taken over, compassion showing only when I needed to use it.

David and I talked late into the night, our newfound cash affording us the ability to go wherever we pleased. Months had passed, and it was nearly Christmas, and he asked me to go with him to Monterrey once again before I headed home. We gathered the crew and told them to have a good Christmas, slung on backpacks heavy with cash, and headed for the bus station.

The buses careened around the curvy roads that spread ahead for miles. I saw many accidents on these pothole-filled roads, blood and metal spewed across the highway. The drivers were reckless and fast, their goal speed and delivery, and with that mindset came lots of consequences. I remember being in a bus accident that was caused by fog. The bus ended up on its side, and I crawled out the window. I remember bodies lying all around. Screams and bloody faces flash across my mind. This time, however, we were delivered to the bus station safely. We climbed out, sixteen years old, and headed to David's home.

My relationship with David, looking back, is a classic tale of two people jostling for power, trying to find space in each other's lives to exist. We had nearly beaten each other to death when we met, circling each other like caged dogs. When I had won the fight, I took up my space as the leader. He rebelled against it, and we butted heads many times. Fragile, precarious though it may have been, our friendship was the best I had ever had. We had remained tied together in this vicious dance of friendship. I was glad to spend a few days with him before going home.

What does it mean to arrive at home after you have been living your life on your own, robbing trains and taking drugs and being a totally different person than your family knows you to be? Surreal.

I eased my way back in and became Toño. Who was I really? Jorge or Antonio? I only knew that I was split in half to the core—two separate, distinct people.

But karma, most often, has a plan. I returned home to visit, this time to a newly purchased tract of land where a house was being built. Save for a few block walls, and an adobe room that had been built first to house everyone, nothing more was accomplished. When I asked why the house wasn't being finished, my stepdad had no answer.

"We didn't have enough money from you," he said, stumbling feebly on his feet.

I was livid. I had sent so much money, enough to be set for the rest of their lives, and he resisted every effort I had made to help better themselves. I felt used and betrayed, but I never mentioned a word of it to him. Did my stepdad suspect? He did. I was wrong for trusting them both.

My mom hugged me, and I looked at my stepdad, sprawled in a drunken pile on a dirty mat lying on the floor.

"We're so glad to see you, mijo," my mom said, wiping tears with the corner of her apron. A new baby brother bounced on her hip—he would be the last. I looked at him and his solemn black eyes and couldn't help but smile. Drool spilled over his lip, and he reached for me.

"Mom, you look tired," I said. She touched my cheek and went back to the soup that was bubbling on the stove. My stepdad stirred on the mat as the little kids ran in circles around me. The two oldest of my younger siblings had started school but went sporadically. They couldn't afford the monthly payment you pay to attend school in Mexico. When I came home, I made a habit of paying their tuition through the end of the year.

"Where's Chucho, Ma?" I asked, stuffing a warm tortilla in my mouth.

"He's with Malena. She's pregnant," she said.

I looked at her and wondered at the sigh in her voice. Why would she deny Chucho a happiness in a life that was hard? He needed someone in his life to make him happy after the life we had led. Malena made him happy.

They were the best cooks, her family. But when I would go to visit my brother, Mom always made me food before I went. "Don't eat anything there," she said, her superstitious ways revealing themselves. I would look at her, hard, and laugh.

Malena had many siblings, mostly sisters. Her mom would look at me carefully. She was hard, yet kind, and said, "I can't read you, Toño. Your eyes are too strong." I always wondered what she meant by that.

In San Marcos, where Malena's family and eventually my brother lived, many dances were held. It's a dimly lit town with pock-marked streets and rough people. I often left there late, the dances ending toward the darkest edges of night, and traveled by taxi back home.

The taxi would drop me off at the very bottom of the street, and I would begin the mile-long walk up to my parents' house. In Mexico at night the darkness is all-consuming. A bleary streetlight here or there does nothing to pierce the black velvet that swallows you. I walked swiftly, one foot after the other, and when I would see the last stretch before my tiny street, a shudder would push through me. To my right was a field filled with corn, dry husks standing sentinel against the black skies. A half mile ahead, I could see my street awaiting my footfalls. I hated this stretch, and always ran it so it would go by quicker.

One night, I approached this last stretch and felt strange shivers course through me. The moon flickered grimly, as if trying to hide its face, and I shoved my hands in my pockets and started walking briskly. A rustling to my right stopped me in my tracks, and I slowly turned my head to peer into the darkness. Seeing nothing, I continued forward, but the rustling in the corn was growing louder, and it stopped whenever I stopped walking.

I began to run. Beside me, the unmistakable sound of someone following me shot through the field. As I approached the street turn-off, now running, a figure came into view and I froze. Leaning against a streetlight was a dark shape. I squinted my eyes to see more clearly. He was lighting a cigarette, and his face was blurry as he lifted the burning embers to his lips. It glowed heavily orange in the hazy night, like the fires of hell from a distance. I stared at him, goosebumps raising high on my arms.

I turned left, my house in view, and whistled for my dog. Oso came at top speed, barking, and the figure disappeared behind me, but I felt him on my neck, hairs on end as I slipped into the gate at my house.

I told my parents the next day what had happened, and they simply nodded their heads. "Nahual," they said, never flinching in their assessment. It wasn't the first nor the last time that stretch held dark things.

I had decided that I wanted to visit Oaxaca, to revisit the place where my memories still lingered. I longed to see my friends there and to reconnect in a way that would tie up the loose ends I felt were blowing in the wind. I said goodbye to my family, as I readily did several times a year, and boarded a bus headed toward the city that had rocked me to sleep every night as a young boy. Trepidation filled me, but I knew that it was something I needed to do. I needed to close a gaping hole that still filled me.

After hours of driving, we dipped into the rugged mountains that surrounded Oaxaca, and my heart lurched at the sight. It was a tug of something that felt like home, yet not quite. I thought of my dad, buried in this state, and a light whisper brushed my neck with thoughts of him and how he had died. I tried not to think of him much, but he crept in, along with the cold fingers of whatever had driven him to his death. Was it murder? Had he taken his own life? I would never really know, and I fought the suffocating darkness that stalked me harder than anything ever had.

I stumbled off the bus and was hit immediately with the smells of the city. A smile crept onto my face. My feet pounded the pavement as I went around the corner where the zocalo greeted me. I was assailed by the brightness of the Oaxaca sky, so clear and full of a sharp blue, and the piercing heat of her day that turned to stinging-cold needles at night. I shuddered, then remembered that I was no longer that small boy alone. I was an almost-man, one who had taken care of himself with no help from others. I had money in my pocket and knew who I was, and I walked into a hotel and rented a room where I had once slept on the patio.

I walked the streets that afternoon, seeking out places and faces that I had known. I asked around at the market, speaking names like Maria, Socorro, Rebecca, and Miriam, friends who had never cared that I was sleeping on the street, a lost boy. Friends who had their moms feed me when I was hungry. You find that those are the friends who stick in your mind, the ones who don't have to care but do anyway. I found that the girl I had always cared for the most, Maria, was now married to a Coca-Cola man, one of those who ride the back of the truck and distribute the product through the streets. Miriam, I was told, had moved the stall she ran with her mom to the Mercado de Abastos. The others—no one knew what had become of them.

I sat outside the school in the same place I had years ago, the sun-warmed stone bench holding me in place. I stared hard at the doors, remembering how my friends had all come spilling out and how my heart would soar. I waited for them every day to be done with school so they could play with me. As I sat and watched, I heard a bell ring, and the doors burst open. Faces passed me, full of the energy that school being done for the day brings, and the whoosh of air from their flying steps hit me in the face. I smiled, but sadness filled my heart; I knew that I could never recapture the feeling of what once was. It was a space in time that was gone. Their faces would stay in my memories now, only to be brought out when I wanted to remember them.

I walked to the Mercado de Abastos, hoping to find Miriam and chat with her about life and all it had brought us. We were still young, still alive.

This market was a vast, sprawling mass of humanity which stretched over several blocks. It was teeming with stalls, ripe fruit, and people haggling over the price of potatoes and meats. It was life at its fullest, the truest place to see people going about their day. I entered and spent time simply walking. When I had been lost, this was the place I went to be around people and feel them walking beside me.

I had been told where to locate Miriam's booth, and it didn't take me long to find it. I pulled up a chair and sat down, willing her to recognize me. They served a variety of dishes at their booth. Delicious carne guisadas simmered in bowls, along with chile rellenos, and big vats of homemade rice with hard-boiled eggs lining the sides of the pot. My mouth watered with the smells of the food as I watched Miriam and her mom serve customers. The thin area between where they served and where people sat was filled with brightly colored plastic plates swimming with food. She plucked a bottle of soda out of a tin tub filled with ice and handed it to the man sitting next to me.

"Hola, Miriam, how are you?" I put out there. "It's me, Toño."

Her eyes looked at me, unfocused for a moment. But connection, though forgotten, runs deep. Her eyes knew me in that second, and a big smile crossed her face.

"Toño! Oh my gosh, is it really you?" she exclaimed, taking off her apron to come around and give me a hug. "We didn't know what happened to you!"

She embraced me long and hard, then returned to behind the counter to keep working. She served me food, and I sat at their booth for the rest of the day, chatting with her as she worked. I told her what had happened to me, that my mom had found me, and I returned home. I also told her of my life, the adventure and the hardship, about the back and forth between countries and worlds, a life she couldn't imagine. It felt good to talk about it with someone who was set apart from that life, someone who could simply hear me.

When she was done working for the day, I walked her home and asked if she wanted to go out with me the next night. She said yes.

I met her the next evening at her house. I was nervous. I felt like I led two distinct lives: one in San Antonio and one when I came back to Mexico. I always believed that my horoscope sign, Gemini, the twins, meant that I had two different sides to me. It allowed me to channel both Toño and Jorge, two distinct personalities that acted in different ways. Tonight, I was Toño, and my head was clear.

I knew it wasn't going to lead to anything, but we went to the movie theater where I held her hand and ate popcorn. Afterward, we walked around the zocalo, ending up at some food stalls, stuffing our faces with delicious tacos and sodas. Then we found a bench where we ate postres out of their crinkly paper and looked up at the stars. We kissed all the way to her home, up against street corners and hidden doorways, and I said goodbye as she went inside to her small concrete home.

In the next two days, I ate my fill of the tropical fruits Oaxaca had to offer and the delicacies I had missed. Then I boarded a bus and headed north. I never saw Miriam again.

19.

Texas called me back, and I was ready to greet her, putting Oaxaca behind me. Each time I crossed the border, coming from either the north or south, I tried hard to tamp down the feelings of leaving. I lived in a vaporous mist between worlds, each one bent on drawing me back under its skin. Someday I would have to choose where my home would be.

Arriving back, I made my way to the semi-trailers continually parked at the fruit market. The sidewalk was uneven as I counted the steps, the gravel crunching under my feet. The open air and the smell of fruit sitting in the sun felt like home. It occurred to me how many places felt like home.

I threw my things into the back and caught the eyes of my friends who nodded and were glad to see me, but I didn't see David. His absence gave me pause.

I gave no thought to Camila, who had stayed out of my mind for the past months I had been gone. I didn't want to go back there. It was hard to see her kids in that situation, and yet I knew she had family that would help her. She had sisters and a brother, and also the tragedy of the murder of her mom and sister. She had seen heartache as well, but she had family, and I wasn't responsible.

Yet, oddly enough, I found myself making my way to her apartment.

My every cell fought the walk up to that door, fought the inexplicable urge to open it and walk inside. I felt outside my body, knowing what I would find would be not what I wanted. I slipped in, the key turning softly in the lock.

In the hazy dimness of the room, I saw one of

my friends asleep on the couch, dreaming away an ugly high, from the smell in the room. He sat up, rubbing his eyes, and looked at me. I looked at him and said, "Where's Camila?"

His eyes widened, and a look of fear passed over his face, still uncomprehending that I was standing in the room. I had told them before I left when I would be home, but I liked to arrive early—always, that element of surprise. My friend pointed upstairs, a single solitary lift of his finger, and I walked up that short flight to the door. I opened it, and the sight settled over me, like a warm blanket you expect at night.

The room was musky, the smells of just-finished sex filling the air. David, the one friend who I had considered true, was sleeping, Camila beside him.

I walked over to his side of the bed. I looked at them, what they had done churning through my head like a freight train. With a light flick of my wrist, I lifted the blankets and pulled him off the bed.

He smacked the floor with his head as Camila shot off her side and scooted on her bottom toward the wall. I could hear her breathing, confused intakes of breath. I felt the rage inside myself, overflowing in its maniacal ascent to reach and pour out into my brain.

I stopped and considered my rage. Was I angry because he was sleeping with her? Or was it because I was about to lose one of the best friends I ever had? He had let his jealousy get the better of him. He had needed to out-maneuver me, and I had seen it in his eyes many months before. There would never be anyone I could trust.

As he stumbled to his feet, I grabbed him by the arm and flung him across the bed. Camila scrambled out the door and into the kid's room, thin screams coming from the door. I reached for David and hauled him up by the neck. Punches, felt deep inside me, connected with his face and lungs. Blows reverberated through my hands and released the betrayal I felt. He had been my best friend.

A spray of red fanned out across the bedspread in haphazard patterns. He lay on the floor, breathing raggedly, his face a bloody pulp. He dragged himself up to his feet and made his way out the door and down the steps. And I let him go.

I could hear Camila crying down near the kitchen, and I walked down the steps, each step echoing through the small apartment. I bit my lip, something I did when madness overtook me, and my fists were clenched at my sides.

David and my other friend were walking out the front door, fleeing my rage. I saw David's eye as he shot a glance at me and ran away.

Camila looked at me as the sounds from the kids in their room finally quieted down. "Please… I'm sorry," she pleaded, voice filled with indignation. "I didn't think you were coming back this early."

Excuses, especially ones that were full of self-preservation, never sat well with me. I looked at her and felt nothing. Any emotion I had for her before, any tiny tendrils that existed, were gone.

I walked over to an ironing board cluttered with clothing and grabbed the heavy iron. I took a butcher knife from the counter and slit the cord in half, throwing the iron into the corner. Then I looked at her, plugged the cord into an outlet, and waited.

She was sitting on the floor, eyes darting up the steps and to the door, plotting escape. I didn't know myself in this moment, but the monster had taken over. My blood ran hot as I drug her by the feet over to the iron cord, close to where I had plugged it in.

Her eyes, still bleary from coming out of a deep sleep, looked at me with wariness. "What are you gonna do?" she screamed. "I can fuck anyone I want." Her eyes blazed black, and I took the hot cord in my hand and place it on her leg, the shock registering in her eyes. I could feel the voltage run up my arm as I held it onto her quivering legs, then pulled it away. She went limp and held her hands to her head as I held the cord in the air, ready for the next touch. I knew what I was doing was wrong, as well as I knew I could never stop her from having sex with every one of my friends. I didn't care.

An image of my stepdad passed in front of my face as I held that cord in my hand. He was smiling, looking at me, telling me I would turn out just like him, no matter what. Pictures of my mom, blood trickling down her face, accused and convicted me. I remembered the times he had locked the door to the white house and made me sleep outside in the cold with the corn rustling and making me afraid. I looked at Camila, a nearly naked mess of tears mixed with black eyeliner, and I unplugged the cord and threw it against the wall.

Sitting down on the couch, I stared stoically at the wall as she got up and attempted to put herself together. She pulled her nightgown down and smoothed the front. Her legs showed sooty black marks and red streaking down her leg. She sat down beside me and said, "I'm sorry, Jorge. I'll never do it again." Her mouth went to the corner of my temple, and revulsion filled me. After all this, she still wanted me. I pushed her away and walked out the door, sorry and knowing what I had done would never leave me.

Trust had become a dividing issue in my life. I had learned that anyone can betray and that to become close was to risk being hurt again and again. David and I were the closest thing to best friends I had ever had, and the sharp betrayal of him sleeping with Camila had been a blow. I sat outside in one of the many wide drainage ditches in San Antonio, the embers from my cigarette falling softly on the concrete. I felt much was slipping away. David was someone I could trust, and he had ruined that part of what we had.

I felt a stabbing pain in my gut; remorse for what I had done filled me. What was I turning into? Someone who hurt people? I didn't want to be my stepdad. I hit the ground with my fists, opening angry red streaks on my hands, and put my head down. *I will never fight over any woman again. I will never hurt any woman again.*

As I walked back to the trailer to go to sleep, I reflected on my life and what I had accomplished. Nothing. I had accomplished nothing. I wanted so much more.

David met me at the corner of the fruit market lot, his face filled with sadness, eyes puffed up like marshmallows. His face spoke volumes, and I brushed past him.

"Jorge, I'm sorry man," he said, as I squared my shoulders and kept walking.

I stopped then, holding thoughts captive in my head, and turned around. "You were my friend," I said.

Revenge is best served cold, and I was on a black ride to nowhere. Nights of jumping fast-moving trains and the stink of coal as it clung to my skin let my wound fester. Never mind that I had let my life sink down to a parade of drugs and girls and stolen merchandise. My mind was sifting through torn-apart friendships, and I wouldn't leave it alone.

I set my sights on traveling to Monterrey, alone, dark thoughts holding onto the wrongs that had been done to me. I arrived in the city, deftly slipping into the neighborhood David had introduced me to, *his* neighborhood. I rented myself a hotel room, small and rough, concrete walls painted a bleary blue, and settled myself in for however long it took.

When we had visited before, he had often introduced me to his friends, smiling and affable, I was the funny, handsome guy. Out on the street, I eased into conversation with them, no one giving a thought to me being there alone. Without David. I attended their dances, the pulse of the beat from the local bands filling my ears and fingertips with electricity, as I led his friends onto the dance floor. One girl I remembered well, a former girlfriend, and another girl, whose face seemed familiar to me. The second girl was early in a pregnancy by a father I did not know. Their eyes took me in, and I knew it would be all too easy to accomplish my task. By the end of the evening, I was in the hotel room with one of them. The next day, I was with the other one. I was a swindler, a cheat, and I had taken all that David had held dear and used it for my own. He had betrayed me, and I had returned the favor.

Both girls wanted me to take them back to San Antonio, to see what exciting things it might hold. They didn't care that I had used them; they wanted to use me as well to travel to where they had never been. But things happen, as they will, and the pregnant girl's boyfriend found out about our tryst.

On the third morning, I was ready to leave. They begged me to take them along, and my mind was racing at the trouble I had begun. I wanted to leave town, my revenge completed, and leave them behind. Shadows of men appeared on the street, and I knew I needed to escape Monterrey— a town where betraying your friends doesn't go unnoticed.

I gathered the girls, my things, and theirs, and we snuck away that evening, a train whistle guiding me and them to a meager freedom. I would never walk the streets of Monterrey again.

For some, alighting on a new path is the bridge to getting out from under your circumstances. The girls slipped into life in South Texas, but I found out that after two weeks they had returned home. I never saw them again. But when I had arrived with them and brought them through rumor and then reality to David, his face was the only thing I remember. It was as if it had melted, permanently, in waves of sorrow down his cheeks. When they disappeared and went home, our friendship dissolved as well.

One night soon after I learned of them leaving, a man approached me in the parking lot of the fruit market. It was the boyfriend of one of the girls, and he was waiting for me with a screwdriver.

"Where is my girlfriend?" he asked, anger seeping hard and dark into his face.

"They are gone," I said. "You missed them. They went back to Monterrey."

He was big and dark and angry at not finding her. He pointed that screwdriver toward my neck and lunged at me. I swerved to his left and rolled in the dirt to avoid the plunge of the tool. His eyes spoke of pain and madness, and we battled for several minutes, my right hand connecting squarely with the small bones of his large face. I was small and swift, never having lost a fight. Yet I knew that what I had done was wrong. Just as I had been given pain, so had I given pain. The adrenaline surged through me as I served him blow after blow.

I turned and ran up the steps into the area above the market and called to my friend. He was tall, very tall, and was from Mazatlán, with a .38 that lay under his pillow. He followed me quickly, and when he saw who I was fighting, his face filled with anger. Their eyes connected, and recognition flickered in their eyes. I had opened a powder keg, not knowing that fights and bullying had occurred while both lived in the streets of Monterrey. My friend had taken much from him, and he wouldn't anymore. He pointed the gun and he fired.

My mouth opened as I saw the bullet enter him near his groin, and he fell back with a thud. He lay in the street, blood dripping into the hard-packed dirt beneath him. I was panting as I looked around, hearing sirens in the distance and knowing there were eyes watching. We ran, knowing that we could return after he was taken away.

I don't know what happened to him, and whether he lived or died. But the air was charged with the scent of something ominous. The fabric of our lives in the fruit market changed after the incident.

David, as well, had disappeared from my life, like an invisible lifeline sinking fast into the ocean. It happened quickly, like the unexpected lopping of a limb, and I never saw him again. Who was I to need friends? I needed no one.

That very night I circled the crew for a massive gathering, white powder smudged under our noses, frenzy pushing us toward the tracks and another night of plunder.

20.

A blur of passing days ran before my eyes. Our stash of stolen items was stacking up in rough boxes of scratchy brown, and the quicker we got rid of them the better. I sent piles of money home to Mexico after we sold the bounty of pilfered goods, feeling good that my mom was getting things I thought she deserved. In every part of society, money is an obvious temptress, a means to an end, and when I would travel to see them again nothing would be built. No new house or running water. Only small portions of the money reached them.

San Antonio is a beautiful city, but to the inhabitants who exist on its west side, it's a mixture of light and dark. Tiny homes dot the streets with Spanish-style architecture, and apartments sit squat and blocky. It's gritty and full of soul, a hard-scrabble life, the place where I made my home. I walked the streets at night, taking in her lights and thinking about what life I had wanted to live. I was far away from home, my hands tight inside my pockets, and on my own like I always had been. Was the money I made from fast-moving trains really mine? I knew it wasn't, but I didn't care. I was riding a bullet that was hurtling straight to the center of nowhere and I didn't want to get off. Life in San Antonio was consuming me, the brightness of it all. I had wanted to hold the world in my hand, but instead it was holding me.

We were now heeding the call of the tracks several nights a week. I had assembled a small group of core friends, but even so, they were friends that I didn't care if I lost. I warned them of the danger brought by this type of life. "It becomes something you can't stay away from," I told them, as they shifted on hesitant feet. But they followed me and soon swung with balance as the cars rumbled down the tracks. It was a provocative mix, as we dissolved tabs of acid on our tongues and let the big moving hulks carry us down the line.

My links to the dark places where I sold the goods we threw off the cars were strong, but they wanted more from me. I had become close to the man in charge. He saw himself in me and knew I could be trusted. But for me, it was a hard choice as I discovered just what it was they wanted me to do. *This is the point that I should stop*, I said to myself; *this is the time*. And as the words stopped short of falling off my tongue, I found myself, late under midnight moon, carrying out their orders. I would do it many times more until I simply didn't. Until their demands were more than I could bear to fulfill.

You can be invisible if you need to be. Lots of

things are possible in this invisible realm that you think aren't possible, and I had learned to be stealthy, quiet, and unnoticed. Do you know that small bump in the night, the one that presses you into a semi-wakeful state but not quite enough to get up and investigate? I am that sound, soft and silent, covertly stepping through your house and rifling through your things. I am the shadow that passes under your window and sits, for hours, watching you and your routine, your day-to-day. I am the one who reports back your every step, to let them know what you do and what you eat, when you shit and what toilet paper you use. You are blissfully ignorant as I slip away as stealthily as a tree sits in a dark forest, and you fall back asleep into oblivion. And if you are on the wrong side of the men in the shadows, you might disappear, all because I told them every movement you made.

And my days passed, with small squares of brightly colored paper dissolving on my tongue, comic book figures and superheroes that melted into slick saliva, sending me into altered reality. This was the order of the day as the light of the Texas sky slipped into dusk.

A major haul had been planned. We had long ago memorized the train routes, and we knew just what cars would hold the best items. I was already sifting through the countless boxes of jeans and shirts meant for department stores, mentally separating them into what would bring the most value. Watches, sports equipment, jewelry — this was highly valued by the men who bought the things we took. They knew where they in turn could sell it. I was building a business plan in my mind.

I went through the steps the night would bring. As we sat preparing, pulling up thick jeans and boots that would protect us when we hit the hot metal of the tracks, I thought about the doors and the lines of train cars that didn't move quickly enough to leave us behind. I felt the acid entering veins and head, exploding in a race to my eyes. As we set out the door, I put one in my pocket for later when I boarded the train.

Shrill whistles pierced the dark as those designated to steal the cars separated from our path. We were stealth and darkness, rolled into the youthful faces of those who had gone without. We were drugs and vitality, and you could see the pain of our mothers who had lost their children to this life, this outrageous life, that brought us riches and loss. My brain was functioning at full capacity, seemingly expanding in its quest for all that I hoped and desired.

As the train yard came into view, we disappeared into the bushes to wait. Wait, as always, for the next thing, the next score, the next hot kiss of anguish, and the tearing away of lips that meant to claim and never could. I was stoic, lean, and I was here. Waiting.

I could hear the train whistles as we crept through the darkness. The wind blew harsh on our backs as one by one we latched onto the train, like a baby that refuses to wean. My hands were steel as, heavy and lilting, it received me into its depths.

Once inside, with the sound of my friends ripping boxes open, I took a moment to place that familiar square on my tongue. I knew I was taking too much. As it dissolved and traveled rapidly through me, I let myself look at the night sky and stars as they twinkled merrily. I swung myself outside and moved swiftly to the apparatus that connected each train. I needed to work my way up the cars to get to several hard-to-open doors. I've never been afraid, or at least, never let myself believe I was.

I jumped and grabbed ahold of the bottom of the car, sliding myself underneath and then shimmying my way the length of it. The underside was rumbling, and the metal felt hot on my hands as the trestles underneath slid by me at an alarming clip. Closest to death was where I thrived, looking it square in the face and telling it to fuck off. This is where I met myself each time, that small boy who wouldn't give up. The boy who had his head smashed against concrete, no single molecule of compassion in sight. This was where I found him and banished sleeping alone on city streets. This is where I overcame.

I swung myself up into the car and began to rip open brown square boxes, pitching each one out of the moving car and watching them get smaller and smaller, turning into dots as they hit ground.

But on paths we believe to have in order, chaos still ensues. In that black velvet night with scrub brush flying by outside, I could feel the train slow down. Its immense bulk jerked and quaked as it rumbled from fast to slow to nearly a stop.

Bells went off in my head, and I looked outside quickly, scanning left and right. Immigration? Cops? I leapt, not knowing where my crew was, and took off scrambling through the hard rocks that had come up to meet me. I was alert, the drug sparking bright synapses, and the sound of a dog in the distance piquing me. I ran, and not fast enough—the animal's breath came hot on my back. I felt teeth wrap around my ankle, and my face hit the dusty ground in front of me, blood quickly spurting from my head.

I turned around and grabbed the dog, one I could see belonged to the authorities, grabbed its neck and swung hard. It landed with a thud and lunged back at me as we fought right there, the semi-arid landscape hard on our backs. I squeezed its neck, the moment overtaking me, until the furry body grew limp and breathed raggedly.

We were both stunned, and as footfalls grew closer and were finally upon us, I started to fade. The stars in the sky grew dimmer and dimmer, still arcing in bright circles as the acid played itself out, blood leaking, until I closed my eyes and gave in to their shine.

I don't know how many minutes or hours I was out, but I came to in the back of a police car. I kept my eyes closed and felt the bruises on my body begin to pulse. My head was a wall of pain. The roughness on my arms from the authorities handcuffing me and placing me in the car was nothing compared to what I had felt at the hands of my stepdad. I liked pain.

I opened my eyes to lights glaring and the night sky slowly turning to dawn. I was alone in the car and looked around outside to see men walking around, surveying the scene. The train sat silent, waiting. None of my friends were there. I didn't know if they had gotten away or were farther down the tracks. I knew I would never give their names and give them away. Their names were safe on my lips. As I passed out once again with the taste of dirt in my mouth, I let myself slowly drift.

Rumbling. I awoke, fully alert. The car was bumping over small backroads to reach the ribbon of highway that snaked itself toward the city. Two agents sat in the car, faces bleary with the night. One turned around and looked at me, curious as he scanned my face.

"Do you speak English?" he asked, as he looked down at a sheet of paper and marked it with a pen. I nodded my head yes, as I knew to never give oneself away as weak. I knew enough to get by. I heard him say, "You're going to jail, my friend." I looked at him hard, no expression, and slowly turned my head to watch the train tracks disappear behind me. The long stretch of landscape was dotted with small, brown boxes that had been heaved wildly.

I had always been in control of my circumstances, moving the strings of my life carefully so not one note would be off-key. This control was born of the disarray that encompassed me, and today it had caught up and tapped me on the shoulder with a bang. Images of my mom flitted across my mind, but I was comforted, knowing I had sent her enough money to last a long time.

I didn't know where we were going, but soon San Antonio came into view, and we wound our way through its streets to the doors of the police station and jail. Menacing, its white concrete gleamed in the morning sun. I was pulled roughly from the vehicle and, still handcuffed, guided inside the walls of the facility.

Once inside, I could see a few faces that I knew. Faces smudged with the grease of the train flitted nervously to me, and I didn't look at one of them. I had taught them that to show fear was to be done.

They took me into a separate room and left me to sit there. Time passed, hours, until someone came in—a fellow Spanish-speaker, who sat down with a yellow legal pad and a drink of water for me. He looked at me with friendly eyes I knew were a put-on and proceeded to get all the questions out of the way.

Who planned these robberies? What is your name? What cartel are you working for? Are you the leader? How many times have you done this? Where are you from? Why would you do this?

I looked at him, my face impenetrable, and didn't answer one of the questions he had asked me. He tried in Spanish and he tried in English, and I gave him nothing. Though I knew I was in the wrong, I wasn't going to make it easy for him. It was his job to find the wrong in me, and I wasn't going to help him. He gave up, hours later, and I was left to sit once again for an indeterminate time.

It was a cut-and-dried case, really. We were guilty of train robbery, but we had not had weapons. My hand, when I took the police dog down, maybe that was a weapon. I felt bad about that, as it made me think of my dog, Bear, who had always been so faithful. But in those fractions of a second, you act, as I had my whole life. As I sat there thinking about everything, the door busted open and two new men came in.

"You really need to be a better judge of your friends," one said. "They've all given you up as the one in charge. El jefe. The boss."

My face showed nothing as I looked at them, but my heart beat fast. Could they be bluffing? I was sure they had to be because none of my friends would give me up. But a tingle at the back of my neck told me otherwise. I should have known that in this world I wasn't safe. Even with those who came from my own country, my name was not safe in their mouths. I looked carefully at the men's eyes and knew them to be speaking the truth. "You're going to be assigned a lawyer and you will be convicted," one said.

Throughout this process, no one was alarmed that I had come into this country undocumented. I wasn't even asked about it. It was an everyday occurrence. You were prosecuted for your crime, had your trial, did your time, and then were deported. The face of the immigration landscape today calls for arrests and cages and riotous roundups, everyone crossing undocumented assigned a day in court. But back then, unless you committed a crime like we had you weren't considered a criminal for being here. You were caught and you were released.

This land was once Mexico, and though the border says differently, we have been moving in and inhabiting this land for hundreds and hundreds of years. When Ronald Reagan signed the amnesty bill in 1986, allowing a multitude of hard-working people to come out of hiding and become citizens, the landscape for the undocumented became even more open. If you believe all that you hear today, then you are not hearing the right stories.

By now I knew there was no question—my friends had betrayed me. I kept my face a stone as they led me out to booking. I knew enough about what was going to happen. I would be photographed, have my fingerprints taken, and be searched.

As I waited in the hallway to be moved, I felt the rough concrete wall behind me. I moved my fingers, each digit, over those walls until they were scratched and bleeding. Along with the dirt and grease from the train and the burns I had received numerous times from the hot metal, my fingerprints were nearly unrecognizable. And when a dirty, disheveled seventeen-year-old kid had his picture taken and fingers were pressed into black ink, what came out of it was a jumbled mess.

The processors looked at me and at my fingers and smirked. "What is your name?" they asked, and the first one off the top of my head, as I spoke my first words since arriving at the jail, was "My name is Javier."

Searched, showered, and placed in an orange jumpsuit and sandals, I walked through the doors and into the Bexar County Jail. My face was a stone, unreadable in every way. I stared straight ahead as I walked through the cold corridor and into a room that held many narrow bunks. Blank faces stared back at me. As the door roughly thudded shut, I laid my head back on the rough pillow and gave myself up to whatever was going to happen.

A lawyer presented himself to me, appointed by the court to get me through the proceedings. He was a nice man and tried to get all the information from me that he could. My English was rough, but we communicated well, with some help from a translator, and he represented me in the best way a public defender could. If you're surprised again that I was given a public defender, do your homework. As humans, we all have rights, especially in the USA. I had no record or history in this country and no paper trail with any name or picture on it. I was Javier.

We were in and out of court many times, with endless conversations, procedures, and talking. I watched as several people testified about their products that had been stolen, representing the nameless companies and stores we had taken from. Officials from the railroad, looking bored and tired, came in and out, and after several weeks I stood before the judge and pled guilty.

I was just another case on the docket for a given Thursday. I was no more or no less than anyone else who had come through the courtroom that day. There were no protestors outside holding signs that told me to get out; there were no government officials giving hate-filled speeches on the undocumented; and the sun shone on me in a cloud-filled sky as they guided me out the door to a waiting van. I had been sentenced to two years in jail.

Was I sad? I believed that I was responsible for what I had done, but I wasn't sad. Life is a series of choices that turn you this way or that. When I had hopped on that bus that took me away from home at six years old, as young as I was, it was that choice that took me away. I had chosen a way that led me to the jail cell I was about to inhabit.

Only later did I find out that our group and our escapades had become notorious in the South Texas area. We had been robbing trains for years and had never gotten caught—until now. My name, *Jorge*, was being whispered in certain circles as someone to be feared.

I left the courtroom and entered the waiting van. It turned north and sped toward inevitability. Suddenly there was a commotion with the drivers, and I turned my head to listen.

"No, that isn't right," said a crackly voice on

the CB. "Turn it around and bring him back."

We had been headed for the federal penitentiary instead of the county jail. My stint inside had just begun.

21.

There are two things you can be in jail: in control, or not. The Bexar County Jail was not a huge jail by any means, but there were enough inmates inside to make it an unruly place. There was no privacy; the cells were set up in group form, ten to fifteen men per room. I let the atmosphere wash over me as I contemplated each face. I still knew who I was inside, but if you think I would let that side of me show, you would be wrong.

It all came down to the separated groups: Latinos, blacks, whites, and all others. As with every other area of my life, I stood on my own. No one had ever guided me in how to interact with others, so I went with my gut. Being surrounded by iron bars and cement changed nothing. I stuck my chin out and began my time.

I never saw my friends again, the ones who turned on me. We had all been caught at the same time, but they gave me up. They were released from custody and deported back to Mexico. Would they come back to the States? Probably, but I would never see David again. His friendship was a hole in my heart for all the good and bad things that had happened. I had loved him like a brother, but he wasn't my brother. He had saved himself, and in doing so, dropped our friendship into an abyss. It let me know, once again, that no one could be trusted; not women, not men, not friends, nor lovers. No one would have my trust again.

Yet I remained an amiable person and people were drawn to me. In a tight space filled with hardened men, I used this to my advantage. I made friends easily, and many of them had heard of me and my crew.

"You're the ones that robbed the trains, ese!" they would say. "How did you do that?"

I spun tales of drugs, dark nights, hot metal, and thousands of dollars in profits. I piqued their interest and could keep them riveted for hours with my stories. I found that telling my stories earned respect.

But my defenses were up, as there were many who did not like me. Falling asleep in our unit, beds lined up with no walls to separate, was something that took getting used to. I lay awake for the first several weeks, like a cat that could see with glowing eyes through the hazy dark, lying in wait for anyone who would try to harm me. My fists were my weapons and I remained ready.

I was a fighter and was ready to use my fists at the slightest provocation. My blood and adrenaline ran high all the way to my hands, and I knew they could cut deep and true. I had learned well how to hit hard with my knuckles because of my stepdad. Feeling knuckles slice through your bones tends to teach you how to use them.

Several weeks in, after much whispering in corners and dark looks my way, one of my unit mates decided it was time to make his move. I had seen him moving around me, trying to scope me out. But I have always been able to see right through people. He was older than me, in for petty burglary, and wanted to maintain his cred throughout the jail. When he made a lunge for me, I was sitting at the table eating, ready and waiting. I moved to my right and he fell, his fist hitting nothing but air as I leapt to my feet to avoid the attack. He looked at me, straightening himself, and wiped the spittle that rested on his lip. And it was on.

A crowd gathered as we went at each other, blows reigning down on each other like raindrops falling heavily on blacktop. We matched blow for blow, falling to the concrete floor. I connected with his cheekbone, my knuckles big, and could hear the crack against stark bone. He fell, and I nimbly jumped on top of him, pounding my fist against his head and gut. In turn, he got a jump on me and hit in places that doubled me over.

I knew that to be who I needed to be in this place, I must finish him. For several minutes more we dodged and punched, the surrounding group growing rowdier with each hit. I wanted to finish it. Leaping onto the table now smeared with spilled food, I jumped onto him and buckled his legs, pinning him in a hold. His breath wavered, voice ragged and rasping, and as he raised his hand in forfeit, I knew I had won—won the day, as well as the respect of everyone there. From that day on, they dubbed me El Tigre, the Tiger, and I found myself at the top of the chain.

A month after entering jail, I became a trustee, and this gave me opportunity to get out of our unit. I delivered mail to inmates, mopped floors, and took a cart around with books, like a small, traveling library. I was happy to be out of the unit. To become a trustee, you must obviously be trustworthy, and they had deemed me so.

As a boy, I had wanted to learn so many things, but my circumstances had prevented me from doing so. I loved reading comics and learning from stories. My schooling had been sparse, a year or two at most, and now the longing in me to know more took over.

There were many resources for the inmates, and I found out that GED classes were available to anyone who wished to learn. I was nearing eighteen and had not had enough schooling, but I wanted to learn English. I showed up for classes and began to learn. It was basically a "learn on your own" class, so workbooks were given to us and the time was spent poring over them. There were also tapes we could listen to, and with each book and tape I finished, my English grew a bit stronger. My goal in life had always been to better myself, to learn and see new places and things. Staying stagnant was not part of who I was, and when I received my certificate saying I had passed my GED, I was proud.

I had taken up drawing as well, and along with paper, we were given solid, white handkerchiefs on which we could outline and color a design. I drew elaborate Virgen de Guadalupe patterns and carefully colored them in. With lots of time to think, I let some of the demons that had always followed me come out in the art I was drawing. Swirling masses of darkness, fangs and teeth bared, took shape on paper and cloth. Religious symbolism ran rampant, and I let it all out. Then I sent them home to my family, hoping they would see me for more than the money I could send them.

At night, as the unit grew quiet and I settled in for another restless sleep, I thought about my family. I had written them numerous letters, but I never heard back from them. What was it I sought? Maybe a kind word that gave encouragement or something that said they were thinking about me. Had I given up the right to encouragement, with all I had done?

In my head, I knew that I was enough, that I

was important. My stepdad despised me for being another man's child. I was a reminder my mom had been with another man, and his hate festered. For my mom, I represented my dad and the fierce love that had existed and been snuffed out. I looked like him, acted like him, and reminded her of him and the other children she had lost. To my little brothers and my sister, I was the one who brought them things; I was a giver. They saw me as someone who came around and the table was bounteous. Their tummies were full when I was around, and I became their father figure.

When could I be me? When could Antonio be who they saw? My heart ached, and I let it, for all the things I knew needed to be remedied in my life. I bore a hole through the jail ceiling at night, letting my thoughts drift upward, leaking out into the dark sky.

Camila came to visit me several times in jail, briefly, enough to stay connected to me. She put money into my account, five dollars at a time, so I could buy cigarettes and other petty things, but being a trustee allowed me access to those, and her help was not expected.

The chipping away of hours spent in solitude, though surrounded by many faces, started to affect me. Today I was sleeping in a jail cell, and many years back I had slept on the open streets of Oaxaca. Two separate prisons? I knew that no matter where I laid my head, I was always free. I hadn't let my time being lost change who I was, as young as I had been. I hadn't let my stepdad and his abuse change me, and I fought to maintain who Toño was. The future was still brilliant before me, and there was enough time to change my path, as I had so many times before. I longed for the day that I could walk out of this cement box and feel the air on my face. When that day came, my life would take a different path.

One day as I was making the rounds with the mail, the guards alerted me to a visitor. It was my attorney. He looked me in the eye and said,

"They're releasing you early for good behavior. They're letting you out."

A feeling akin to pain thrummed in my chest. My path was crooked, but it was still mine, and mine to change. As I finished out the last days, having been inside for eight months, I said goodbye to many friends I had made. "I'll find you when I get out, Tigre," they would say; and I knew I would never see them again. I functioned better alone, not giving away bits and pieces of myself to anyone. I hated when people clamored for me and my attention; I didn't want it, and I didn't look back when I left.

They loaded several of us onto a bus that sped southward to the border where we would be deported after serving our time. While we drove, I sifted the time spent inside the squat block building. Eight months is enough time to sort through whatever may be troubling you. I had gotten too big, my name drifting through many lips and telling many tales that were too big for me to handle. I became well-respected in jail as well, but I didn't want this life. I didn't want to be the jefe, the boss, known for being a successful robber of trains or handler of drugs. Why did I keep pursuing it? What demons were chasing me, breathing hot on my neck? I remembered the hard place I laid my head at night when I was little, and I knew that God was with me in that place. His warm breath had chased away any demons that sought to take me under their wing. I had lost him somewhere along the way.

We arrived at the border, somewhere in the dusty town of Laredo. I leapt off the bus, slinging my backpack across my shoulder, and turned around to nod slightly to the guard who had traveled with us. He nodded back, and I turned to cross the bridge, the waters of the Rio Grande sparkling beneath me. My thoughts flashed to the many times I had crossed that river, so young, yet knowing it was the thing I needed to do. I thought of people I had lost to bad decisions and worse timing. I had slipped through the knots that life had tied for me, unscathed and unharmed. But my soul had taken a beating, and it needed to heal.

The air was just a bit sweeter than it had been yesterday, and as I crossed into the land of my birth, I could sense a change coming. I didn't know when, but I knew it was coming and that I would be ready for it.

22.

I made my way southward by bus, having earned $28 in jail over eight months. I arrived in my town, happy to be there, yet saddened that I had never heard from my family the entire time. I steeled myself to greet them, knowing my mom would have been disappointed to know I was in jail at all. But she was still my mom, and as I entered the gate, she dropped everything to greet me, tears spilling over her cheeks as she lay her head on my chest. It was always this way, this coming together in a heady mix of sorrow, regret, and joy at seeing my face. I whistled for my dog, but he didn't appear, and my mom told me he had passed away. Tears stung my eyes and I hung my head. I was inconsolable. To this day I can't get let go that he may have died waiting for me to come home. My brothers and my sister were filled with excitement to see me, and I reveled in family and let the past months slip away. Even my stepdad, who never smiled when he saw my face, was cordial enough that I could meld into their lives for a short time.

I was stunned to find, though, that all the money I had sent home had not been used to finish the house. The bare bones of unfinished rooms blinked back at me nakedly, and I looked at my stepdad with a careful eye.

"Pa, why isn't the house finished?"

He stumbled around, saying many words that didn't quite come together in explanation. "Your cousin brought us the money you would send, but it was never enough." I knew I had sent much, enough to have the finest home on the street. Where had the money gone? I was so happy to be home and out of jail that I watched him as he stumbled away, drunk once again, and I knew exactly where all the money had gone.

Mexico greeted me with smoky outdoor fires and bubbling pots of beans, warm faces, and girls who seemed unusually happy to see me. I let them all in, the warm rhythms of life lulling me into a sense of normalcy. Breakfast of hot coffee and warm homemade tortillas let me catch up with my mom and my older brother. I began to relax, as much as I could let myself, and I breathed deeply of the scent of Mexico.

I began seeing several of the girls who showed interest in me, all at the same time, easily falling into patterns that brought me pleasure and no pain. Faces of current girlfriends and ones from years past faded away as new ones took their place, and I would walk with them and feast at small taco stands, the juice of the salsa running down our chins. I would kiss them, none of them knowing about the other, and promise them the world as I spiraled downward into earthly comforts. I wanted nothing more than to relish time not spent stealing from train cars and tripping on drugs, time away from the cold cell that had held me these many months. This was normal; I needed normal. I let it take me in, warm hands and blissful ignorance. I would meet one girl in the morning, one in the afternoon, and one in the evening. It was a spiral into indulgence, and I didn't care. Jail had let me know that I wanted more, that I needed to change my life. But just as when I was small and lost, I was constantly looking for love and acceptance. I let all the feelings in and their feelings out, satisfying only myself once again.

But when the tug to leave started poking me in the side, I heeded its call and said my goodbyes, leaving everyone as easily as I had said hello. My brother Chucho came to me, busy with his own small family.

"Toño, are you okay?" he asked, concern etched on his face. "We wish you would stay."

I looked at him and said, "Chuy, this is my life.

This has always been my life."

I saw the worried brow of my brother and knew it would be this way forever, the tug and pull of two separate places that I called home. He had wanted to be my protector, the one to save me when I was lost, because he felt that he had been the one to lose me. His guilt was forever on his mind.

"Don't worry, carnal," I said. "You don't have to worry about me anymore." All the horrors we had experienced together conveyed as we looked at each other, his face so similar to my own. But it was okay. This was how our lives were to be, forever separated. We hugged swiftly and I turned to walk away, leaving my family and my mom as I always would to make the trek north, where lay the other half of the string connected to my heart.

Buses, trains, and hard-packed roads later, I arrived at the border—three months after I had been deposited there by the prison bus. Going back to the USA had never been in question. My other life was there, and I was determined that I would make my years count no matter what I went through to get there. Work in Mexico was scarce, and I had ties and connections in the north that I would not let be severed. It was my other home, and I would be damned if I would spend eight months in jail to let myself stay in Mexico, suffocated by a family who had never had me to themselves.

Nuevo Laredo greeted me as it always did, with its dusty streets and hard-scrabble people. Border towns were a tough place, filled with people who had seen much. I ambled around for a day or two, eating my fill from the ill-lit taco stands late at night, getting a feel for how crossings were going. Was there much border patrol presence? Were people getting rounded up?

You are nothing if you're not prepared, which is why so many get caught. The coyotes who cross you for a price are predators, only in the game for the dollars they can make. They gouge you for thousands when, for small moments of preparation, you can do it yourself. I had always crossed solo, never depending on others for my safety. The sorrow and hope seen in the scraps of refuse left behind on the banks of the Rio Grande tell a story that can never be felt except by those who experience it.

My crossings signified a shattering of boundaries, a chaos contained and controlled by me. When I first entered the United States, it was because I was young and it was an adventure. Now, I felt a purpose; no walls or rivers or invisible borders would keep me out. I slipped into the cold water and glided across to the dusty banks that had come up to greet me so many times before. I pulled myself out and dried off. Clarity filled me, and I moved softly in the dark night, catching a train headed north.

I slipped into the city like I had never left her, taking my place on the west side, in the Alazan Apache Courts. I sought out work. I wanted to stay away from the trains, needing to direct myself in a path that would be beneficial. I didn't want to stay at Camila's anymore, couldn't stay there. Her sister offered me an empty bedroom in her home for a small fee, and I accepted.

I did not want to start anything with Camila again or give her a reason to think I did. Sometimes she would come around, and we would all smoke weed together. We kept our exchanges civil, but I could see in her eyes that she still wanted me back. I had my own things to take care of, and her possessive need of me was not something I wanted to face. Her sisters and brother loved me like their own, and it was hard to break away from them because they felt like my family. But I needed to set myself straight.

The San Antonio streets held me and knew me, tucking me under their wing as their own. The city never spit me out, the dust-lined streets laid out evenly under the Texas sky. I was illegal, as the times called us, *undocumented* a better word. There were many of us out there looking for jobs, always working hard at what was put before us. I was desperate to stay away from what I had done to put myself in jail, even though I knew it was easy money, something I could do without ever thinking. It took more courage to try and stay on a narrow path.

Nearing my eighteenth year, I met Peter Campos when I was looking for work in the aisles of a home improvement store. Peter was kind and funny, and he smiled as he said, "You need work? I've got a house being worked on right now. Let's go." We drove to his home, and there I met Don Wicker. Peter introduced us and we clicked.

The purposeful rhythm of painting and construction thrummed inside me, and I dove right into the job. Don became the mentor that I had never had, and his handyman and painting business was the model I would use when I later started my own painting business. He lived in a house near downtown San Antonio with Peter, his partner, and his home was a wonder to me. An older structure, he had bought it for very little when the area was not a sought-after place to live, and he had turned it into an oasis. He was a craftsman and a hippie and made beautiful art that inspired me. He was eclectic and driven, yet able to rest and relax in in his backyard, with a joint in one hand and a beer in the other.

Don put me to work painting houses and digging fence posts, and he taught me how to run a business as a self-employed owner. He saw my worth, and it made me work harder. Being undocumented meant nothing to him. I was the best worker he had ever found, and he taught me, like my uncle had, to work hard and play when the work was done. In the mornings, he would beep outside my window, and we would head to work. He never failed to stop at a tiny restaurant that served the best breakfast tacos in San Antonio. From their tiny kitchen and four-table dining area, they piled enchiladas with spicy sauce and melty cheese, Tex-Mex flavors that I learned to love as much as authentic Mexican meals. We would laugh as the workday went by, often taking breaks to smoke a joint. These days were carefree and pleasant, and when the workday was over, we would sit in the jungle of his backyard and drink, our bodies resting from the hot sun of the day.

He had been with his companion, Peter, for a long time. He had been born and raised in Georgia, leaving when he discovered it was not an accepting place to live as a gay man. He moved to Texas. Peter was a teacher from San Antonio, and they connected and became a couple, happy and full of enthusiasm for life. They treated me like their own son and absorbed me into the daily fabric of their lives. Hard work, mayhem, and zest for daily living were what they showed me. "Always get the job done first, Jorge," Don would say. "Then get the beer out and start the party!"

Jobs came and went, sometimes sporadic, and when those slow times came, we would work in his garage. I would clean it and arrange his tools the way he liked, then he would begin work on pieces that he made for local art galleries. He created coffee tables with wooden cacti and snakes he had cut and hand-painted with dazzling designs. He sold them on consignment to make extra money, and many times I would go along with him to drop off pieces.

"Jorge, you shouldn't be living over there in the courts on the west side," Don and Peter would tell me, naming the government housing I stayed in at Camila's sister's place. It was the only place I had ever lived inside. Most of my earlier years in San Antonio had been spent inside the empty trailers at the fruit market. I would just smile and slowly draw in the sweet, acrid smoke of the sweet herb in front of us, and we would laugh well into the night before I headed home to the small room I called my own.

I was diligent and worked hard to keep my head above water, to not let it sink down where it once had been. I split my time between working with Don and spending time with my other friends, because even though I had lost many to betrayal, I had many that remained. I was still

Jorge. In certain circles where our train adventures had become legend, they spoke my name with fear.

I wanted peace, but the temptation to dip back into that life was strong, and after a long day working, I would come home and slip cocaine into my nose, the power surging greedily into my veins. I could never totally lose myself and be who I wasn't, but the coke allowed me a diversion from something I knew I was missing. Drip, drip, drip, like the acid Don, Peter, and I sometimes took, letting ourselves free fall into the void.

I swung wildly from Don to my friends that lived on the west side of the city, doing different things with different people. The way out was still cloudy. I felt good about the work I was learning, what Don was teaching me. But going back with my other friends and slipping into an easy incoherency was a step back, a metal-studded whip that caught me coming and going.

Some weekends, to maintain my sanity, I slipped away from everyone and took a day to myself. I would ride the bus to the fringes of the city and find a mall where I could lose myself. There I would eat food-court pizza and watch a movie, letting the effects of too many drugs fade away to a dull roar, a tapping on the skull if you will, dulling with each minute. Riding back into the city, I would get off at the River Walk, meandering slowly around each bend, refreshing my mind and keeping it sharp.

On many nights, I found myself stalking the train yard, planning and prowling. The night would surround me, thick and black, and I would fight the terrible urge to taste the rails once again. It was easy for me—easy money, easy life, raking in money to live and send home. But I fought hard against it, more than anything I had ever done before. I remembered my time inside and didn't want to risk going back. I also didn't want to risk re-establishing the dark connections I had made. My time was done, and I was free. Even though they hadn't come after me, I believe that they simply didn't know where to find me.

I kept a low profile and made several trips back to Mexico during this time. I brought back friends from my town, Ricardo and Moco, who wanted to experience life in the United States. We talked on the way to the border and up through Texas, about what I had done on the trains, the money I had made. I could see the flicker in their eyes.

"It's rough, carnal," I said, looking them over carefully. "It's not easy."

Ricardo answered, "We could send money home and keep a lot for ourselves. We would be rich." Their smiles went down deep, and I just tucked my arms around myself, as I watched the landscape speed by as we rode the train into the city.

I walked downtown to Market Square, friends in tow, to where Camila had made a scene when I was a younger. I liked to come here and dance, to get lost in the swirl of warm arms and pliant lips. Downtown San Antonio is alive, with lights strung outside that create a cozy atmosphere where you can lose yourself.

The night was warm, and as the beat swayed, my eyes met a girl. She was younger than me, and her name was Marta. She didn't know who I was or my reputation. I asked her to dance, and we twirled under a night sky. Breathless from exertion, we sat down, and I watched as my friends learned the dance steps, tapping merrily on the cobblestones. I learned that Marta lived on a tree-lined street in another section of San Antonio, where I soon found myself visiting several days a week. But very soon after I met her, I found that she didn't like to have just one boy for her affections, and my heart quickly turned cold.

Her sister Teresa was a year older than her, and she came to me, shyly, and apologized for Marta. She told me that she had always liked me. And to get back at Marta, I took up with Teresa, perpetuating the cycle of my life. Teresa, too, was beautiful. It drove Marta crazy that I was with her sister. Their mom was brazen and loud and full of life. Along with her trucker boyfriend, we would go out and party at the local bars. She didn't seem to mind that I was older than her daughter, and she was wildly lenient with us.

Don didn't approve of Teresa. "She's no good for you, Jorge," he would say, rubbing his beard in the way that he always did when he was upset. His face held the smirk that let me know he cared. "Forget about her. Let's have a Fourth of July party tomorrow," and his eyes twinkled as Peter laughed loudly in the background.

Work sped by that day, and that evening we readied for a party. The next day, the house was filled with many of their friends, lawyers, accountants, gay and straight. We mingled, and I learned to know many of them as they peppered me with questions about my life. How had I come to be here? Where is your family? Tell us more. My English, although passable, was not good, but I tried to tell them a bit of my story. I was happy meeting Don and Peter's friends.

The party migrated to a rooftop where the beer flowed freely. An Independence Day parade was passing by in the streets below, and I remember the day being unbearably hot. The conversation grew lively and heated the more drinks we downed. I kept thinking about Teresa and was also still thinking about Marta; and oddly, I remember that my hair had blonde tinges on the tips.

An argument broke out between me and the guy I was talking to, an altercation that was fueled by alcohol and ignorant questions, questions that were not okay to ask. He took a swing at me.

"What the hell are you doing?" I screamed, my anger taking over. I knocked him clean out. His nose poured blood, and my fists were clenched as I bit my lip in a drunken rage. Don pulled me back and held me until my anger had cooled.

We apologized to each other. A lady who was good friends with Don—I remember her telling me she was a lawyer—sat down with me. And as we chatted, the evening cooled as tempers did as well. We dove deep into conversation.

Aside from the fighting, the day and the party

had been what I needed. Don knew when I needed to step away from the pettiness of my love life.

Don grew busy, and jobs were coming in fast and furious. He asked me if I had anyone who could come and help work for him, to form a crew. I thought that Paul, Camila's brother, could use the work, so I brought him with me the next day. Don was going to drop us off at the job, but as usual before we started, we took whatever drugs he had on hand. Don was a firm believer in allowing drugs to enhance whatever project you were working on, so out came the acid. Don dropped us off and drove away to the other job.

I set up the job: ladders, brushes, and drop cloths spread out. We began painting, cutting a sharp edge with paint into the building as I had learned to do first with my uncle and then with Don. I was becoming acutely adept with a brush and roller, learning the trade quickly.

The sun, though, shone hot on our faces, and suddenly, my fingers and hands were too big to hold the brushes. I looked at Paul, up on a ladder with no experience in painting, and wondered why the walls of the building seemed so high. Wavy, the sky was wavy and moving, and we looked at each other and began to laugh endlessly. The brush strokes grew long and unending, and the bursts of laughter grew thick and loud inside our heads. Our tongues were dry, and the words we spoke came out in high-pitched garbles, unintelligible to anyone around us.

A tree was growing close to the building we were painting, and it cast a long shadow on the walls. I couldn't get the paint to cover the shadow. It couldn't be covered. I somehow found a chainsaw and began to cut pieces off that tree. The shadow wouldn't disappear, and I kept cutting and hacking with the chainsaw while we laughed into the heat of the day, the acid filling up each cell until it burst in massive waves through our bloodstreams. Don arrived and I was still cutting that tree down, trying to make the shadow disappear so we could paint. He was furious.

"What the hell happened here?" he yelled, looking at the furious streaks and marks of paint on the wall.

"The shadow. I couldn't paint around the shadow and the tree had to go," I said, blinking.

Don gave me the blackest look and held open the door, and said, "Get in the fucking truck!"

Paul and I looked at each other, dissolving in fits of laughter. We loaded the truck and drove away, and to this day, I'm not sure if we ever finished that job.

23.

The days blended into months and suddenly years. I now thought of my life as before and after jail. My whole body yearned to go back to the way things were, to the rush of the wind on the train as it carried up and over my face. What was I doing to accomplish anything in my life? It took every cell of my body to stay upright, work straight, not give in to the lie that said the dark shadows were more exciting than the light.

I remembered being small, lost on the cobblestone streets of Oaxaca, when a warm coin I held in my palm was deposited in the church offering. I had made a deal with God: *If I give you all I have, will you save me?* He had saved me, yet all I wanted to do was mire myself in drugs and women. I wanted to be back on top of my game. I wanted to be the most dangerous man I could be. I was giving in to a pot-and-cocaine-filled haze, longing to be someone I didn't yet know I wanted to be.

I found myself sitting again on the edge of one of the many large drainage ditches scattered throughout San Antonio. The sun was setting, and I lay back against the warm concrete. The waning light brought shadows that surrounded me, and I looked up at the pinkish streaks left in the sky.

"What is it you want me to do?" I said to a silent echo. "Please send something to save me." And I closed my eyes.

Don left me in charge of small crews, and we painted many projects in the city. I gained knowledge and experience each time. I valued what he taught me. I knew I could use it in the future.

I had brought several different sets of people over the border from Mexico, never losing one in the crossing. They were men and women filled with dreams of making it big here; some succeeded, and some headed back home within weeks. It's a vicious cycle, the push and pull of leaving your homeland and the aching poverty that propels you to do anything you can to make enough for your family.

I had begun to care for Teresa. Our times together were good, but she, too, wasn't satisfied with just one person to make her happy. We had been off and on for a while. One day, as I walked up to her house, I found her talking closely with a guy, heads bent at familiar angles and her chin cocked toward him. I knew then that I had to be done with her. She told me she had been with him, that I had to deal with that. I gathered my stuff and headed back to the west side, where the streets narrowed and gathered me into their cracked sidewalks and weed-filled side streets. She would try to get me back, but I was done. I was twenty years old.

My room at Priscilla's, Camila's sister, was small. The block buildings that made up the Alazan Apache courts were all the same, squat and plain. I liked things neat and orderly, so my cologne bottles were lined up on the sparse dresser the way I liked them. My clothes were folded neatly into piles, separated by shirts and pants and placed carefully inside the drawers. I had several silver rings with me from the times I had pickpocketed in Oaxaca. Sometimes I held them in my hands and thought about the people I had taken them from, if they even noticed they were gone. They were beautiful, inset with turquoise and topaz, and I wore them when I went out on special occasions. A small silver dish held them, set carefully beside the colognes; I liked looking at them.

It had been a long workday, and I was tired. Outside my door and down to the kitchen, I could hear Priscilla and her kids making noises and settling down for the evening. The smell of weed filtered under my door as I lifted small hand weights, blue jeans from work still on, in front of a mirror. I didn't want to smoke tonight. I looked at myself in the mirror and saw a man, black hair falling from a center part, with eyes that had seen more of life than anyone should before the age of twenty.

Outside my small window was an even smaller balcony where I stood sometimes to smoke a cigarette and view the lights of the city. I heard a beep outside the window and some yelling. I didn't go check because living so close to everyone in this part of town means there's always commotion outside. Always the sirens, the people yelling and fighting, and rowdiness on the sidewalks. I kept lifting my weights.

"Jorge!" came the voice from under my balcony. "Are you there?" I walked to the window and opened the small doors that led out, throwing on a jean jacket for the night air. It was Rafa, the kid down the street.

"Que quieres?" I said, with little interest.

"Orale guey, come down, I have someone I want you to meet," he yelled back.

Rafa lived with his large family in one of the Habitat for Humanity houses that had been built at the end of the street. His mom, Juliana, worked at the local soup kitchen, and I knew her from volunteering there several times. I don't think she liked me much, as she seemed to think I had been dealing drugs. Rafa had been in trouble with the law after several of his friends burned down a house and a child had been killed. He had been forced to turn on them as a witness and had to go into hiding when he testified against them. I had come to know him enough that he asked me if I could stay with him while the police put him in protective custody at a local hotel. We stayed there several weeks, eating food the county paid for and watching lots of TV. After that terrible incident and case was over, I sometimes went to his house and we lifted weights outside on his patio. He looked up to me.

But tonight, I didn't feel like meeting anyone. My English was still not good, so I answered him in Spanish, "No, estoy cansado. No quiero. I'm tired. I don't want to."

He laughed and said, "Come on, there's really someone you need to meet. Just come down for a little bit."

I could see a car parked out front with several people inside, and I sighed and told him to hold on. I didn't want to meet or talk to anyone tonight. I wanted to finish my weights and slip into bed. Instead, I put my shoes on and moved through the house. Priscilla looked at me from the couch, music videos playing Spanish pop that flooded the room. I opened the door and went down the steps to meet Rafa on the lawn.

"What's up, man?" I said, hoping this wouldn't take long.

"Come to the car, just come," he said,

scurrying away before I could say no. I followed him over to the small car that idled at the side of the curb. He was waiting for me on the opposite side.

In the front seat, I could see his friend Lisa, whom I had met at his house not long back when we were lifting weights. She was very nice, with a ready smile, and worked at the Inner City soup kitchen and aftercare with Rafa's mom. She said hello and flashed a smile.

I turned my head to the backseat where another girl sat. I didn't need to meet another girl.

The interior of the car was dark in the waning light of the day, but I could see she had dark brown hair, and as she turned her face to look up at me, Rafa said, "Jorge, this is who I want you to meet. This is Melissa."

I've always said during my toughest of times that God was watching over me. He fed me when my belly cried with hunger, put people in my path to help me know I wasn't alone, and never took his eye off me when I was in the darkest pits of hell. When Melissa stuck her hand through the window to shake mine and smiled at me, something stirred—something I couldn't quite place.

"Say her name slowly. She likes to hear the accent," said Rafa, laughing.

I leaned partway into the window and said slowly, in my thickest accent, "May-lee-sa." Her face lit up and she threw her head back in laughter that went right through me.

"Let's go for a ride," said Rafa. "Come on, go put a shirt on."

I backed away from the car and ran inside, my heart beating swiftly, startling me. I threw a shirt on, some cologne from the bottles so neatly lined up, and ran through the house to go outside.

"Where are you going in such a hurry?" Priscilla questioned, my urgency a signal to perk up and take notice. I looked at her and smiled and ran out the door.

I climbed in the back of that tiny car and scooted next to Melissa. Lisa and Rafa laughed in the front, turning around as we sped through the darkened streets of the west side. I turned to look at Melissa and wanted to talk to her so badly, but afraid of how my English would come out.

She smiled, and I said, "Do you want something to drink?" She shook her head yes, and we pulled into a gas station, where Rafa and I hopped out.

"Who is she, man?" I said to him, and he just smiled.

"She's Lisa's friend. They're on some mission here through the Mennonite church," he said. "They're both from Ohio." Ohio was a state I wasn't familiar with, and I thought he meant Iowa. Rafa said, "It's freaking cold up there, dude. You'd freeze your ass off."

We got back in the car and drove aimlessly as Melissa and I glanced at each other and smiled shyly. The lights of San Antonio were a backdrop to every single sensation that was coursing through me, like tiny drops of glitter had dropped into the night sky.

We pulled into Roosevelt Park around 11:00 P.M., bottles of soda in hand, and I got out and asked her if she wanted to walk. The others stayed behind as we began to loop our way around the darkened, tree-lined space. My tongue grew thick with words, tangled in and around the English I had tried so hard to learn. She looked at me and simply smiled, and I felt at home in the moment; the silence for once not an enemy to me. Her frame walking so close beside me made me feel alert. I stopped walking and took her hand, looking straight into her eyes, confused by what I was feeling. I wasn't this way around women, unsure and unsteady.

And no sooner did the words "Can I kiss you?" tumble out of my mouth than our heads were bent and leaning into each other as if all oxygen to breathe had been cut off until that very moment. There was no expectancy in her kiss, just the giving into the moment for what it was.

I drew back from her and knew that she was different, so unlike any other girl I had been with.

Her face had no ulterior motive or aim, just to be in the moment we were in.

We found a picnic table near an empty basketball court and parked ourselves there to talk. People have asked me many times, "What did you talk about? You didn't know English!" I don't have an answer for them. She angled her head and listened to me, really tried to understand what I was saying to her. She didn't laugh at my pronunciations, but tried to take it in, to tear it apart and hear me. She spoke as well, trying the small fragmented words she knew in Spanish, to communicate with me as best she could. Her hair shone under the park lights, and we shared more than one kiss as we sought to understand what we were feeling. We were in a bubble, a small bubble in time, and when Rafa and Lisa found us, it was nearing dawn.

As we drove back to my apartment, I put my arm around her, not sure if or when I would see her again. I climbed out of the car and we parted, and I walked inside to lie down and sleep, until

Don beeped the horn for work at 7:00 A.M.

As we rattled to work, I wondered if I had dreamed the whole night. A white girl from the north who made me feel very tangled up inside. What had come over me? Don grew quickly annoyed at my tiredness and lack of concentration. I didn't want to tell anyone just yet what had happened. I wanted it for my own, a small secret gift that I held unwrapped in my lap.

Four days, then five days went by, and I asked Rafa several times about her, trying to play it cool, like I didn't really care.

"I don't know, man. I haven't seen Lisa in several days," he said. "I'll see what I can find out."

I decided that I didn't care, that I wouldn't let myself fall. Something about her was different, though, something that I couldn't lay down. I pictured her face as I walked out the door of Priscilla's the next day, on my way to Rafa's after work. Camila was at the bottom of the steps, coming over to see her sister, and I hesitated but kept walking.

"Hi, Jorge," she said shyly, putting a quiver in her voice that I caught immediately. "I've missed you." At this point I wanted nothing with her, but our past was intertwined like a woven length of rope.

"I'm good. On my way out right now," I replied, smiling, yet hurrying to move past the steps.

"You look different," said Camila, her eyes boring into me like a drill. "Have you met someone?"

I kept walking, picking up a bike that one of Priscilla's kids had left carelessly on the lawn and hopping on, its banana seat hugging me to it.

"Hey!" Camila yelled after me. "Who is she? I'll kill her!"

Her words echoed through the block buildings that sat silent as I pedaled down the sidewalk to the end of the street.

I reached Rafa's house in minutes and wheeled my way up to the fence that surrounded their home. His mom was outside, and I chatted with her, asking politely if Rafa was home. She smiled, as she had warmed up to me lately. Rafa came out and opened the gate, and we stood there talking, the air cool as the evening spread about the city. San Antonio had become my home, but I knew it wasn't where I would make my home.

The dusk was spreading as a car came slowly down the road and pulled into their driveway, shutting its lights off with a click. I saw one person get out, saw that it was Lisa, and my heart did a little flip. Was she alone?

I still sat astride the bike as Lisa came up to the gate to talk to Juliana. I waited while she greeted them, and then she turned to me and smiled.

"Hey, Jorge," she said. "Melissa is in the car."

I turned and saw the shape of her sitting in the front seat. The blood rushed to my face. I rode the bike over to her window, feeling like a child for being so anxious. I said, "I didn't know if I would see you again."

Melissa opened her mouth to speak, then shut

it again.

"I wanted to see you, but was scared," she said.

My mouth went dry as she struggled for words, and when she looked up at me, stammering to help me understand, I leaned in and kissed her. I wanted to erase her fear. I wanted to tell her of my own. I wanted to tell her everything until I couldn't talk anymore. She got out of the car, and we looked at each other, an arm's length away.

I had wanted someone to see my darkness. One night of talking to her and I knew she would drive away the shadows. I knew she would fill those spaces with light instead.

I felt her fingers brush through my hair and down my back and knew I had found my solace. God had sent me someone to help save me from myself.

Epilogue

She looked in the mirror, cheeks blush pink, and pulled the veil down over her face. She'd always wanted to use a wedding veil, wanted that moment of him lifting it up and seeing her eyes—fully seeing her—something she had always dreamed of. She didn't care how hopelessly romantic it sounded. She pictured his dark brown eyes and the way he held her chin when he kissed her.

She heard the words that had been said in her ear, well-intentioned but tone deaf: "But are you sure?" She thought about the looks people gave them, rolling the meaning around in her brain, and brushed it all stubbornly away. Loving someone is never as clear-cut as people think it should be. Sometimes you close your eyes and jump.

And she walked down the aisle, where he was waiting to hold her hand with his warm one. And they said *I do.*

Printed in Great Britain
by Amazon